International
Energy Agency

Energy Policies of IEA Countries

The United Kingdom

2012 Review

INTERNATIONAL ENERGY AGENCY

The International Energy Agency (IEA), an autonomous agency, was established in November 1974. Its primary mandate was – and is – two-fold: to promote energy security amongst its member countries through collective response to physical disruptions in oil supply, and provide authoritative research and analysis on ways to ensure reliable, affordable and clean energy for its 28 member countries and beyond. The IEA carries out a comprehensive programme of energy co-operation among its member countries, each of which is obliged to hold oil stocks equivalent to 90 days of its net imports. The Agency's aims include the following objectives:

■ Secure member countries' access to reliable and ample supplies of all forms of energy; in particular, through maintaining effective emergency response capabilities in case of oil supply disruptions.

■ Promote sustainable energy policies that spur economic growth and environmental protection in a global context – particularly in terms of reducing greenhouse-gas emissions that contribute to climate change.

■ Improve transparency of international markets through collection and analysis of energy data.

■ Support global collaboration on energy technology to secure future energy supplies and mitigate their environmental impact, including through improved energy efficiency and development and deployment of low-carbon technologies.

■ Find solutions to global energy challenges through engagement and dialogue with non-member countries, industry, international organisations and other stakeholders.

IEA member countries:

Australia
Austria
Belgium
Canada
Czech Republic
Denmark
Finland
France
Germany
Greece
Hungary
Ireland
Italy
Japan
Korea (Republic of)
Luxembourg
Netherlands
New Zealand
Norway
Poland
Portugal
Slovak Republic
Spain
Sweden
Switzerland
Turkey
United Kingdom
United States

The European Commission also participates in the work of the IEA.

International
Energy Agency

TABLE OF CONTENTS

List of figures, tables and boxes

FIGURES

TABLES

BOXES

1. EXECUTIVE SUMMARY AND KEY RECOMMENDATIONS

EXECUTIVE SUMMARY

Since industrialisation, the United Kingdom has relied heavily on fossil fuels for the bulk of its energy supply. This is by and large still the case today, but change is coming.

Mounting evidence of potentially damaging anthropogenic climate change has prompted political parties to broadly agree on the need to decarbonise the energy system. The government has laid out ambitious targets for reducing carbon emissions up to 2050 and mapped pathways to a low-carbon future. Greening the economy is seen as an opportunity for creating jobs and growth. As public expenditure remains severely constrained in the coming years, the government aims to catalyse private sector investment in new infrastructure and in energy efficiency.

Since the last IEA in-depth energy policy review in 2006, the United Kingdom has defined a strategy to move to a low-carbon economy and to tackle climate change with a remarkable sense of coherence and commitment. Climate change has become a clear priority in energy policy and the country has set unilateral legally binding targets for reducing greenhouse gas emissions by 50% by 2027 and 80% by 2050 from 1990 levels. The IEA recognises the significant level of ambition in the United Kingdom's efforts to reduce emissions.

As with any ambitious unilateral climate policy, it will only remain politically sustainable over time if other countries move, too. The government is well aware of this and is at the forefront of promoting international action both in the European Union and outside. The government should continue its multilateral work to develop firm and appropriately integrated international carbon-pricing signals over a time-frame sufficient to adequately inform investment decisions and reduce investment risks. The interaction of the planned electricity market reform with the European Union Emissions Trading Scheme (EU-ETS) merits particular attention.

LOW-CARBON ELECTRICITY

The electricity sector is a focus area of the decarbonisation efforts. The government has clearly indicated its intent to deploy three low-carbon technology pathways: renewable sources, nuclear power and carbon capture and storage (CCS).

As part of its EU obligations, the United Kingdom must obtain 15% of its final gross energy consumption from renewable energy sources by 2020, more than four times the share in 2010. Electricity is expected to contribute most to meeting this target, although the country has also introduced incentives for heat and obligations for transport fuels. This incremental power generation will be primarily wind, although biomass will also have a significant role; the United Kingdom has a significant wind resource and is already the world leader in installed offshore wind power capacity. In government estimates, wind power generation would increase by 65 terawatt-hours (TWh), or more than sevenfold, from 2010 to 2020, which in practice means erecting several thousand wind turbines on- and offshore, building the network connections for them and ensuring that other forms of power supply or demand reduction are available when wind does not blow. All of this has stirred a lively debate about cost and public acceptance.

Nuclear energy provides 16% of electricity supply. Three consortia have plans to invest in new nuclear capacity, as existing plants are ageing. New nuclear build is to be financed and operated by the private sector without public subsidies. The challenge for nuclear energy in the United Kingdom is economic rather than political or social. Potential investors are now waiting for the government to detail its support policies for low-carbon power generation.

The United Kindgom is globally among the most committed supporters of the development and deployment of carbon capture and storage (CCS). It has pledged GBP 1 billion for projects targeted at commercialisation of CCS such that it can be deployed in the 2020s. The country also hosts some of the most active academic institutions on CCS worldwide. The IEA recognises the significance of UK efforts in this area and encourages the government to maintain its commitment despite the challenging financial conditions. The IEA also encourages the government to continue to increase investment in energy research, development, demonstration and deployment in general to match the country's ambitious climate policy objectives and its world-renowned academic institutions and capability.

All in all, the government acknowledges that to decarbonise the power sector without risking security of supply, new support mechanisms are needed. It has therefore decided to reform the electricity market.

ELECTRICITY MARKET REFORM

A critical challenge faced by all IEA member countries is how to ensure continuing reliability of electricity systems while promoting timely decarbonisation of electricity supplies. In the United Kingdom, around 12 gigawatts (GW) of coal and oil-fired capacity and 7 GW of ageing nuclear power capacity are scheduled to close by the end of this decade. Combined, they account for a fifth of the country's total capacity. Current policies may deliver an outcome that would fail to meet the United Kingdom's long-term climate policy targets, as new capacity is primarily gas-fired. An efficient mix of new, cleaner generation, more efficient use of existing infrastructure and more flexible demand will be needed. Ofgem, the energy-sector regulator, estimates that around GBP 110 billion needs to be invested in plants and networks.

The United Kingdom is ahead of most countries in both recognising the low-carbon investment challenge and attempting to find concrete solutions to it. This is demonstrated by the level of ambition in the electricity market reform (EMR). The detailed reform plans are now being finalised and the government expects the primary legislation to be enacted in 2013. The EMR comprises the following four policy instruments to encourage investment in nuclear and renewable energy and CCS:

• A carbon price floor (CPF) to provide a transparent and predictable minimum carbon price for the medium and long term. This will increase the competitiveness of low-carbon technologies over time. The EU-ETS does not currently provide the price incentives needed for such investments.

• A "contract for difference" feed-in tariff (FiT CfD) to provide low-carbon electricity generators with a guaranteed price throughout the period of the long-term contract. If the wholesale electricity price is below the price agreed in the contract (strike price), the generator will receive a top-up payment to make up the difference. If the wholesale price is above the contract price, the generator pays the surplus back. The design of the FiT CfD will be tailored for different generation types (nuclear, renewable, CCS). The FiT CfD requires a robust and cost-reflective reference price which reflects market fundamentals and is not subject to undue manipulation. Efficient price formation through liquid and deep financial markets will be needed to ensure that this instrument delivers cost-effective results. However, high levels of vertical integration in wholesale markets raise some fundamental concerns about where this condition will be met in practice.

• A capacity mechanism to ensure sufficient system flexibility is available to maintain reliable supplies, especially during peak periods, as the amount of variable and inflexible low-carbon generation increases. This will involve contracting with a diverse range of flexible resources, including generation, demand-side response and storage, which will be managed through a central auction process. The capacity mechanism, too, will benefit from efficient wholesale price formation through a liquid market.

• An emissions performance standard (EPS) to limit how much carbon new power plants can emit per unit of electricity generated. It will initially be set at a level equivalent to 450 g CO_2 per kilowatt-hour (kWh) for all new fossil fuel plants, maintaining the government's commitment that all new coal-fired power plants will require CCS facilities.

In addition to introducing these four instruments, the government also intends to develop complementary policies to help clarify the role of demand-side response, storage and interconnection, and the development of a smarter grid.

The EMR proposes a transitional, targeted intervention to rapidly restructure the technology mix while simultaneously maintaining security of supply. In many respects it represents a fundamental departure from the market-based principles that have underpinned UK energy policy over the last two decades, reflecting concerns that market-based incentives may not be sufficient on their own to meet the government's electricity security and decarbonisation goals.

The combination of interventions proposed is untested. They will need to be carefully monitored and adjusted to ensure that they complement market-based incentives for timely, efficient and innovative private sector responses, and do not become an expensive and ineffective substitute for them. That said, there may be a compelling argument in this case for adopting measures to help maintain electricity security, while accelerating the transition to meet the government's short-term decarbonisation goals, especially given the ongoing delay in establishing strong market-based carbon pricing signals under the EU-ETS.

Given the risks and the need for decarbonised electricity systems to ultimately become financially viable and suitable, the EMR should be viewed as an interim measure, with the ultimate goal of creating a more liberalised market where low-carbon generation technologies can compete to deliver innovative and least-cost outcomes. Where possible, transitional mechanisms should maintain a competitive character and be non-discriminatory between low-carbon technologies. The government has been clear that this is its vision for the EMR and that they will use competitive methods during this transition period as soon as they are viable.

The EMR ultimately relies on continuing public support, and consequently on broad political support. It is therefore essential that public discussion on the reform process be well informed. Currently, it appears that there is support for the need to diversify generation sources so as to provide the dual outcome of increased energy security and reduced emissions. However, investors are likely to ask themselves how enduring the new policies will be if resistance to rising costs is to increase in the future. The government should therefore continue to communicate, in the clearest manner possible, what pathways are available to achieve energy security and decarbonisation goals and their costs. Inclusive consultation processes are essential to encourage widest possible support and ownership of the reforms among key stakeholders and the community.

More in detail, the package of three measures for low-carbon price support (CPF, FiT CfDs and EPS) is more than is strictly necessary, and provides a "backstop" against underperformance of one of the policies. For example, if the EPS and FiT CfD policies are effective, the only additional minor effect of the CPF would be to influence the operation of existing plants; if the CPF is robust and enduring, it can be expected to gradually raise the electricity price and reduce the benefits of the FiT CfDs and possibly render the EPS redundant. This built-in redundancy will raise implementation and compliance costs and magnify potential risks arising from unintended interactions. The government will need to monitor implementation carefully and should be willing to adjust or discard elements that prove counter-productive in practice.

While the three EMR instruments outlined above are aimed at reducing carbon emissions, the capacity mechanism is intended to ensure security of supply. From an investor point of view, the proposed changes to electricity market arrangements may create uncertainty and risk, which may add to the cost of new investment and discourage efficiently timed and sized investment responses. Given this risk, there may be a case for some form of transitional capacity mechanism to help address any lingering concerns. In general, however, IEA experience (Australia, Nord Pool) suggests that a well-functioning energy-only market provides an effective means of delivering the efficiently timed, sized and well-located generation investment needed to develop a competitive, dynamic and innovative electricity sector at least cost.

Over time, the combination of FiT CfDs for all new low-carbon investment and a capacity mechanism for new flexible resources creates a situation where the system operator (or other designated body) may be involved in contracting for virtually all new generation, with the wholesale market playing a diminishing role in investment decisions. In a more heavily regulated market, the burden of delivering the expected policy results would fall increasingly on the government and the regulator, and the power companies could be rationally expected to increase lobbying pressure on them. The government may wish to consider whether this is the permanent direction it desires for the electricity sector, or whether to view the FiT CfD and the capacity mechanism as means of providing certainty during a transitional period of rapid change and uncertainty. If the latter, then the government should provide some clarity around the transitional period, including more detailed guidance on phasing out assistance and moving to more market-based arrangements.

Encouragingly, the EMR will be complemented by Ofgem's efforts to increase the liquidity of the wholesale financial electricity market. Six vertically integrated groups dominate power generation, and in particular supply, in the United Kingdom and therefore have a limited need for financial contracts to manage trading positions and risks. As a consequence, the British wholesale financial market is rather illiquid, and this forms a barrier to entry for potential new suppliers. Lack of liquidity and depth in financial markets also affects efficient price formation with the potential to distort efficiency incentives with regard to investment, operation and end use, but it also reduces the cost-effectiveness of the FiT CfDs and the capacity mechanism which rely on efficient wholesale pricing to help determine strike prices.

To drive open the market, Ofgem proposed in February 2012 to oblige the six vertically integrated groups to sell 25% of their generation in a range of different products in the spot and forward financial markets. This is a welcome proposal that may increase liquidity and depth in financial markets, which could support more efficient price formation and new entry by helping independent suppliers to procure power and hedge their positions more effectively. This has the potential to increase competition, product innovation and consumer choice.

ENERGY EFFICIENCY

Energy use per unit of GDP in the United Kingdom is one of the lowest among the IEA member countries, reflecting both the large share of services and the small share of energy-intensive industry in the economy, but also improvements in energy efficiency. Energy supply and use have peaked, but there is significant potential for higher efficiency, in particular in the building sector.

Ambitious minimum performance requirements (in terms of carbon emissions) for new buildings were introduced in 2010 and will be gradually made stricter so that by 2016, all new-built dwellings will be zero-carbon. The IEA welcomes these improvements.

As around two-thirds of the building stock the United Kingdom will have in 2050 already exists, the government is right to strongly focus on the existing buildings. The tool for this will be the Green Deal. It will enable private firms to offer consumers energy efficiency improvements to homes, community spaces and businesses at no up-front cost, and recoup payments through a charge in instalments on the energy bill. The government is encouraged to define the details of this innovative programme without delay in order to be able to launch it as planned in autumn 2012. It will also be important to establish clear guidelines for monitoring and evaluating progress.

The Green Deal will be primarily a financing tool. For it to be successful, the general public needs to be aware of the potential benefits it offers. Awareness raising is particularly crucial, because the retrofitting work will largely be done by the private sector, potentially including utilities which, at the time of rising end-user prices, may not always enjoy the full confidence of the general public. The government should therefore continue and intensify efforts to raise awareness of the benefits of energy efficiency retrofits and pay particular attention to informing the public of how the Green Deal will work.

Another major initiative is the roll-out of smart meters which is intended to deliver a range of benefits to gas and electricity consumers, energy suppliers and networks. Starting in 2014, a mass roll-out of smart meters should result in 53 million units being introduced to all households and small businesses by 2019.

In the transport sector, EU regulations on the CO_2 emission limits for new passenger cars and light-duty vehicles will start to bite later in this decade, and domestic measures to promote ultra low emission vehicles will complement them. Fuel and vehicle taxes, although primarily introduced for generating tax revenue, are high enough to encourage energy efficiency. The government also has plans for high-speed rail and low-carbon public transport.

OIL AND GAS

Energy policy challenges are not limited to curbing energy-related GHG emissions. Security of supply merits continuous attention. The UK context is that of declining domestic oil and natural gas production. The country has been a net importer of hydrocarbons since 2005 and domestic production is expected to decline by half from 2010 to 2020. The United Kingdom has taken commendable steps to encourage exploration in its continental shelf to decelerate this trend and would likely benefit from seeking more stability in the upstream fiscal regime to promote continued investments.

Oil imports are well diversified and oil stocks are very robust, but the outlook for growing import dependence would merit an analysis of the benefits for creating a Compulsory Stockholding Obligations Agency with a clear supply resilience remit.

Investment in natural gas import infrastructure has been significant to balance the declining domestic production, and import capacity today exceeds annual demand by a wide margin. Recently, liquefied natural gas (LNG) has overtaken pipeline gas as the main means of importing gas, the country's main fuel. This adds to system flexibility and increases security of gas supply, as does the liquid and well-functioning wholesale market.

The United Kingdom is likely to need a range of new infrastructure investment to maintain security of gas supply in light of growing import dependence and changing patterns of gas demand. This will include reinforcement of the transportation system to accommodate more volatile gas supply and demand, particularly as gas plays a larger role in providing backup to wind power generation. It will also include a mix of storage and supply infrastructure to replace declining domestic production and provide flexibility.

KEY RECOMMENDATIONS

The government of the United Kingdom should:

☐ *Maintain its long-term ambition to reduce domestic greenhouse gas emissions and continue its multilateral work to develop firm and integrated international carbon-pricing policies.*

☐ *Take steps to encourage the necessary private investment in energy infrastructure by developing and maintaining stable long-term regulatory frameworks that ultimately support the efficient operation of well-functioning markets.*

☐ *Finalise, to this end, the electricity market reform proposals with a view to reducing uncertainty and encouraging efficient, innovative and cost-effective outcomes, including facilitating integration with the European market; closely monitor and regularly evaluate performance during the implementation of the reform to ensure an effective outcome.*

☐ *Address the need to increase competition among electricity market players and to strengthen market-based arrangements, including introducing arrangements that would encourage the timely deployment of more innovative and cost-effective low-carbon generation technologies.*

☐ *Finalise the work on the Green Deal as soon as possible, as the programme has the potential to significantly improve energy efficiency in buildings; raise public awareness of the benefits of energy efficiency, in particular as a means to overcome economic challenges.*

PART I
POLICY ANALYSIS

Figure 1. **Map of the United Kingdom**

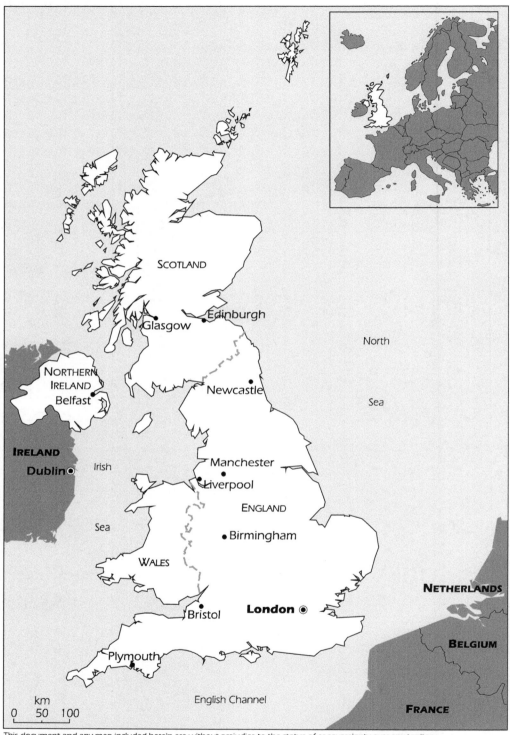

This document and any map included herein are without prejudice to the status of or sovereignty over any territory, to the delimitation of international frontiers and boundaries and to the name of any territory, city or area.

2. GENERAL ENERGY POLICY

Key data (2010)

TPES: 203 Mtoe (natural gas 42%, oil 31%, coal 15%, nuclear 8%, renewables 3.7%), -8.9% since 2000

TPES per capita: 3.3 toe (IEA average: 4.9 toe)

TPES per GDP: 0.10 toe per 1 000 USD GDP (IEA average: 0.15 toe per 1 000 USD GDP)

Electricity generation: 378 TWh (natural gas 46%, coal 29%, nuclear 16%, renewables and waste 7%)

Electricity generation per capita: 6.1 MWh (IEA average: 9.5 MWh)

Inland energy production: 149 Mtoe, or 73% of total primary energy supply

COUNTRY OVERVIEW

The United Kingdom (Great Britain and Northern Ireland) has an area of 244 000 km². The island of Great Britain consists of England, Wales and Scotland, while Northern Ireland borders on the Republic of Ireland (see Figure 1). Over the past decade, the UK population has increased by more than 3 million to reach 62.3 million in 2010. Population is expected to continue to grow, largely as a result of immigration.

The economy is dominated by services, accounting for around 78% of gross domestic product (GDP) in 2010. Banking, insurance and business services are particularly strong and London is a major international financial centre. Industry provided around 22% of GDP and agriculture around 1%.

The UK economy experienced a long boom from 1992 until the international financial crisis in 2008. GDP dropped by 4.4% in 2009, but turned to a 2.1% growth in 2010. The government has adopted an ambitious seven-year fiscal tightening programme to shrink the country's largest-ever peacetime budget deficit (10% of GDP in 2010). GDP per capita is slightly higher than the OECD average. The unemployment rate in late 2011 was 8.4% of the labour force.

The United Kingdom is a parliamentary democracy with a constitutional monarchy. Following 13 years of Labour party rule, the Conservative-Liberal Democrat coalition government led by Prime Minister David Cameron took office in May 2010. The central government has granted a varying degree of legislative autonomy to Scotland, Wales and Northern Ireland (devolved administrations). Energy policy is a reserved matter for the national government, but a number of mechanisms are matters for devolved administrations.

Since 1973, the United Kingdom has been a member state of what today is the European Union. In energy policy, EU law sets requirements for the United Kingdom and other member states in a wide range of areas, including electricity and natural gas markets, emissions of greenhouse gases and air pollutants, energy efficiency and renewable energy.

SUPPLY AND DEMAND

SUPPLY

In 2010, total primary energy supply (TPES) in the United Kingdom was 203 million tonnes of oil equivalent (Mtoe). This is 10% below the historical high of 226 Mtoe in 1996 (Figure 2). TPES in 2009 was 197 Mtoe, the first time the level was under 200 Mtoe since 1984. TPES is on a decreasing trend, with an average decline of -0.9% per year in the last decade. The government projects this trend to continue until 2020 and reduce total primary energy supply by 13%.

Natural gas dominates energy supply in the United Kingdom. It accounts for 41.9% of TPES (85 Mtoe). Natural gas overtook oil use in 1997 and has played an increasingly important role as a fuel for electricity generation and space heating.

Figure 2. **Total primary energy supply, 1973 to 2020**

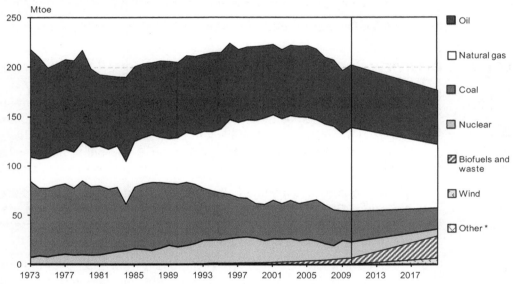

* *Other* includes geothermal, solar and hydro (negligible).

Sources: *Energy Balances of OECD Countries*, IEA/OECD Paris, 2011 and country submission.

Oil is the second-largest energy source. It accounts for 31% of TPES (63 Mtoe). The volume of oil use has been in slow decline over the past decades. Coal contributes 15% to TPES (31 Mtoe). As depicted in Figure 2, the outlook is for a significant decline in the use of coal in the near term. This mainly follows on from adapting to EU air pollution legislation.

Nuclear energy accounts for 8% of TPES. The amount of nuclear energy is expected to decrease over the next decade, as power plants are reaching the end of their operational lives.

Compared with other IEA countries, the United Kingdom has a rather high share of fossil fuels in its energy mix and among the lowest share of renewables (Figure 3). Biofuels and waste represent 3% of TPES, wind 0.4% and hydro 0.2%. The government expects renewable energy supply to grow strongly to 2020: biofuels and waste by 14% per year and wind power by 22% per year.

Figure 3. **Total primary energy supply in IEA countries by source, 2010***

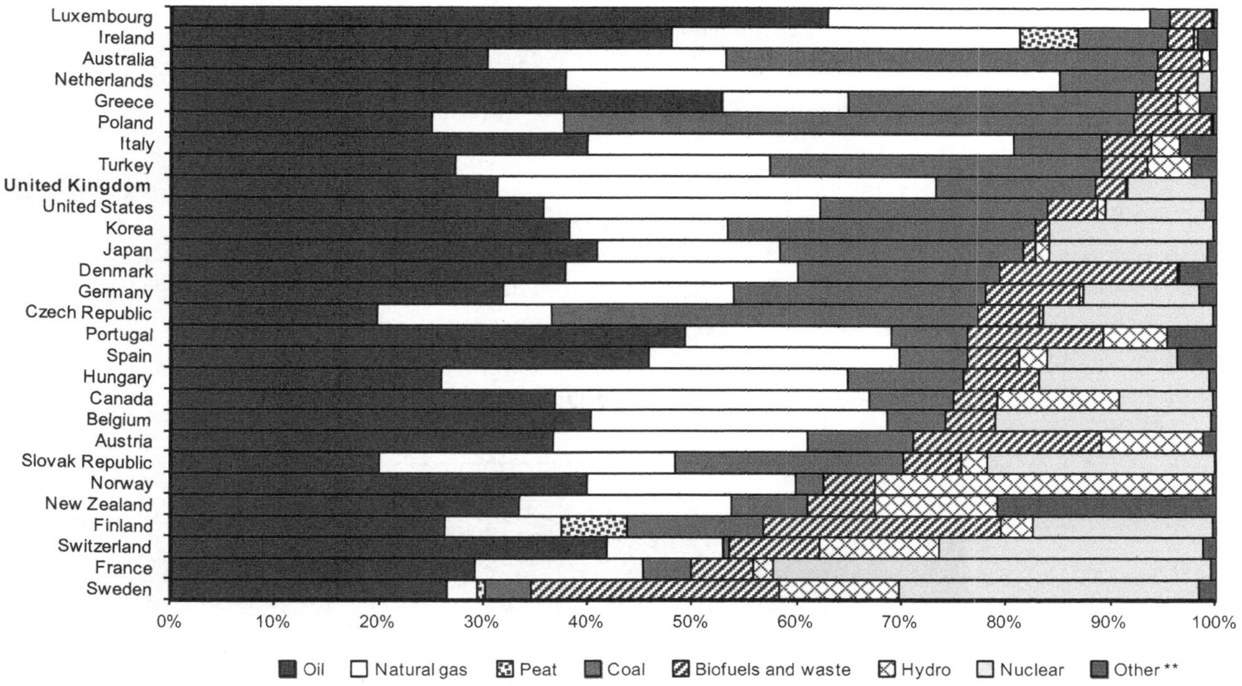

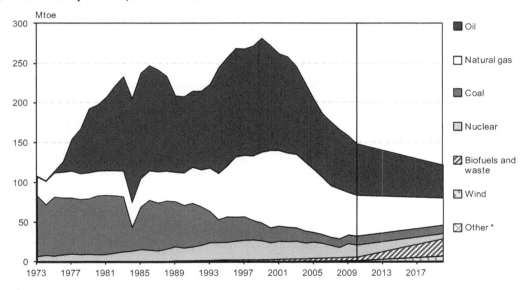

* Estimates.

** *Other* includes geothermal, solar, wind and ambient heat production.

Source: *Energy Balances of OECD Countries*, IEA/OECD Paris, 2011.

Figure 4. **Energy production by source, 1973 to 2020**

* *Other* includes geothermal, solar and hydro (negligible).

Sources: *Energy Balances of OECD Countries*, IEA/OECD Paris, 2011 and country submission.

In 2010, domestic energy production amounted to 149 Mtoe (Figure 4). The United Kingdom imports 30% of its energy supply. Fossil fuel production has peaked in all fuel categories and is expected to decline gradually. Energy supply and production by source is discussed in more detail in Part II of this review.

DEMAND

In 2010, total final consumption (TFC) was 138 Mtoe, up 4.9% from the previous year and comparable to the 1990 level (Figure 5). Oil is the largest energy carrier in the United Kingdom, accounting for 41% of the final energy mix. Next is natural gas with 34% and electricity with 20% of TFC in 2010. Coal accounts for 2% of TFC, biomass for 1.6% and heat for 1%.

Figure 5. **Total final consumption by sector, 1973 to 2020**

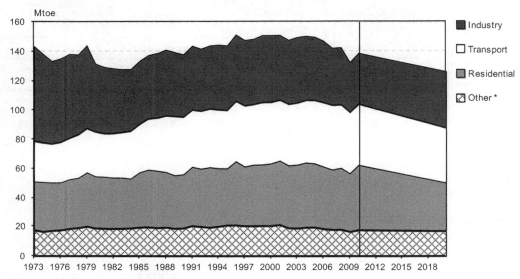

* *Other* includes commercial, public, service, agricultural, fishing and other non-specified sectors.

Sources: *Energy Balances of OECD Countries*, IEA/OECD Paris, 2011 and country submission.

The residential sector is the largest end-user. It accounts for 32% of total final consumption of energy (45 Mtoe). Transport is the second-largest, with 30% of TFC. Industry accounted for 25% in 2010, and commercial and other sectors for 13%. The government projects TFC to decrease over the next decade, driven by a decline in consumption in the residential sector. Final energy consumption is discussed in more detail in Chapter 4.

ENERGY INTENSITY

Energy intensity (total primary energy supply per unit of gross domestic product adjusted by purchasing power parities) in the United Kingdom has decreased by nearly a quarter since 2000, a faster pace than the IEA average. In 2010, the United Kingdom had low energy intensity at about 0.10 toe/1 000 USD GDP. This is a third lower than the IEA average of 0.15: only four IEA countries have lower intensity. The United Kingdom's low energy intensity is partly due to its economic structure, where industry represents only slightly more than a quarter of total final energy consumption, a much smaller share than in most IEA countries.

Figure 6. **Energy Intensity in the United Kingdom and in selected IEA member countries, 1973 to 2010**

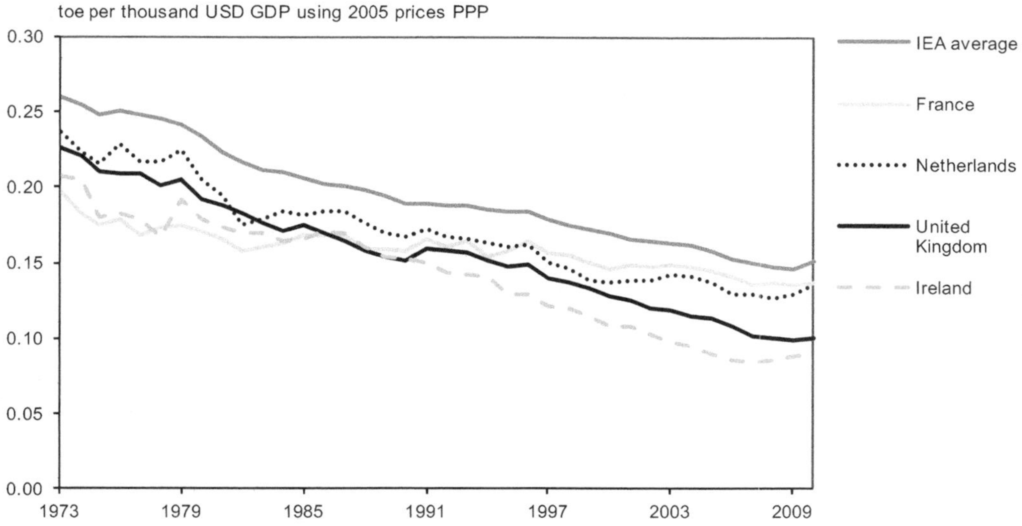

Sources: *Energy Balances of OECD Countries*, IEA/OECD Paris, 2011; *National Accounts of OECD Countries*, OECD Paris, 2011.

INSTITUTIONS

The **Department of Energy and Climate Change** (DECC) was created in 2008 by merging energy policy and climate change policy into one department. It has overall responsibility for the government's energy and climate change mitigation policy. DECC works with a wide range of organisations, both within and outside of government, and is also responsible for several non-departmental public bodies, including the Nuclear Decommissioning Authority and the Coal Authority.

Other departments with major energy-related responsibilities are **HM Treasury** (tax policy), the **Department for Communities and Local Government** (housing), the **Department for Environment, Food and Rural Affairs** (sustainable development and the green economy, environmental protection and pollution control), the **Department for Transport** and the **Department for Business, Innovation and Skills.**

The **Office of Gas and Electricity Markets** (Ofgem) regulates the gas and electricity networks and the competitive markets in gas and electricity supply and retail. The protection of consumer interests lies at the heart of the regulator's role, including those interests in reducing greenhouse gas emissions and security of supply. The regulator is independent from the government, accountable instead to Parliament, in order to separate regulatory decisions from political control and so provide greater long-term regulatory certainty and to encourage market entry and investment.

KEY POLICIES

GENERAL

The government outlined its general energy policy goals in the July 2010 Annual Energy Statement to Parliament. The political parties broadly agree that the energy system needs to be transformed to become more secure and low-carbon. With severe constraints on public expenditure in the near term, the government aims to catalyse private sector investment in new infrastructure and in energy efficiency by developing a clear, transparent, long-term policy framework. In energy policy, the government focuses on the following four key areas:

- Saving energy through the Green Deal and supporting vulnerable consumers. Reduce energy use by households, businesses and the public sector, and help to protect the fuel-poor (see Chapter 4).

- Delivering secure energy on the way to a low-carbon energy future. Reform the energy market to ensure that the United Kingdom has a diverse, safe, secure and affordable energy system and encourage low-carbon investment and deployment (see Chapter 10).

- Managing the country's energy legacy responsibly and cost-effectively. Ensure public safety and cost-effectiveness in the way nuclear, coal and other energy liabilities are managed (see Chapters 6 and 9).

- Driving ambitious action on climate change at home and abroad. Work for international action to tackle climate change, and work with other government departments to ensure that the United Kingdom meets its carbon budgets efficiently and effectively (see Chapter 3).

SECURITY OF SUPPLY

The government policy is to ensure that the United Kingdom's energy supplies are of the right quality, reliable, secure and can provide for future demand. Ensuring that energy supply is secure means working both in the short term, so as to minimise the risks of any unplanned interruptions, and in the long term, by having the right policies in place. This includes policies that encourage:

- open, transparent energy markets, both domestically and internationally;

- diverse energy sources;

- international energy dialogue; and

- timely and accurate information to the market.

DECC is required to publish an annual report (the statutory security of supply reporting requirement set out in Section 172 of the Energy Act 2004). This report provides a technical assessment of the outlook for the supply of electricity, gas and oil up to 2025, drawing on analysis by the government, National Grid, Ofgem and others.

CLIMATE CHANGE MITIGATION

The government's approach to avoiding the risk of dangerous climate change has at its heart the Climate Change Act 2008, which requires:

- cutting GHG emissions by at least 34% by 2020 and 80% by 2050 below the 1990 levels;

- setting and meeting five-year carbon budgets for the United Kingdom during that period; and requiring that those carbon budgets be set three budget periods ahead – so that it is always clear what the country's emissions will be for the next 15 years – and setting the trajectory towards the 2020 and 2050 targets.

The fourth Carbon Budget (covering 2023-2027) was set in law in June 2011, requiring reductions of 50% from 1990. The December 2011 Carbon Plan sets out sectoral measures intended to deliver the Carbon Budget targets.

MARKET REFORM

In July and December 2011, the government published proposals for reforming the electricity market. The proposals are designed to strike a balance between the best possible deal for consumers and giving existing players and new entrants in the energy sector the certainty they need to raise investment. Specifically, they are designed to ensure that low-carbon technologies become a more attractive choice for investors, and adequately reward backup capacity. The government has proposed the following four key instruments for electricity market reform:

- A carbon price floor (CPF) to provide a transparent and predictable carbon price for the medium and long term, something the EU-ETS cannot currently provide.

- A "contract for difference" feed-in tariff (FiT CfD) which is a long-term contract for stabilising revenue and reducing risks to support investment in all forms of low-carbon electricity generation.

- A capacity mechanism to ensure sufficient reliable and diverse generating capacity to meet demand as the amount of intermittent and inflexible low-carbon generation increases.

- An emissions performance standard (EPS) to limit how much carbon fossil-fuelled-power stations can emit.

The government is finalising the detailed reform plans and expects the primary legislation to be enacted in 2013.

INFRASTRUCTURE PLANNING

As discussed above and later in this review, the UK energy system is foreseeing significant restructuring, enhancements and expansion. Like in other countries facing the same transition, this restructuring process comes with the need for sufficient infrastructure planning in order to:

- ensure customer protection while maintaining energy affordability;

- ensure public acceptance of the foreseen changes;

- minimise effects of the new infrastructure on the population;

- ensure the targets of environmental protection are met;

- ensure a transparent and reliable infrastructure planning framework for project developers; and

- ensure infrastructure deployment in a timely manner.

A major tool for ensuring that all these targets are met in England and Wales is the 2008 Planning Act. The Act streamlined the application process, focused the discussion about national needs and gave stakeholders an improved option to be heard. Scotland has devolved powers for consenting energy infrastructure, albeit under UK legislation, the Electricity Act 1989.

The Planning Act sets a threshold for major energy infrastructure to be dealt with, which includes all:

- electricity generation stations above 50 MW onshore or 100 MW offshore;

- electricity lines at or above 132 kilovolts (kV);

- large gas reception, LNG and underground gas storage facilities; as well as

- cross-country gas and oil pipelines and gas transporter pipelines.

With the implementation of the Planning Act, a suite of six National Policy Statements (NPSs) on energy infrastructure have been introduced, debated and approved by the House of Commons and designated by the Secretary of State on 19 July 2011. The NPSs set out the need for energy infrastructure and provide guidance on how decision makers should consider applications for development consent for energy infrastructure according to national energy policy. Local planning authorities should ensure that their development plans are in line with the NPSs.

There are six NPSs with one overarching NPS (EN-1) setting out the government's energy policy, explaining the need for new energy infrastructure and instructing the Infrastructure Planning Commission (IPC) on how to assess which one impacts in a common way. The following five NPSs (EN-2 to EN-6) are planning documents for each specific form of infrastructure, on:

- fossil fuel generating stations (EN-2);

- renewable energy infrastructure (EN-3);

- gas supply infrastructure and gas and oil pipelines (EN-4);

- electricity networks infrastructure (EN-5); and

- nuclear power generation (EN-6).

Besides dealing with policies for energy infrastructure, the NPSs give decision makers guidance on the potential significant impacts of specific infrastructure that should be assessed. These cover potential environmental, social and economic benefits, such as the project's role in the overall infrastructure need or job creation and in potential adverse impacts at national, regional or local levels, such as air quality and emissions, visual appearance, noise, health impacts, biodiversity or related infrastructure requirements (*e.g.* grid connection or upgrades for a power plant).

Major infrastructure projects that are subject to the EU Directive 2011/92/EU on the Assessment of the Effects of Certain Public and Private Projects on the Environment, also called the Environmental Impact Assessment (EIA) Directive, must be accompanied by an environmental statement that sets out the potential significant effects and their mitigation. In addition, it is encouraged to include in all project proposals a consideration of alternatives to the project and their effects. The NPSs also set out how the government's policy on new power plant projects to be "carbon capture and storage-ready" should be applied.

The Planning Act 2008 set up the Infrastructure Planning Commission (IPC) as an independent body, in order to examine applications for development consent orders for nationally significant infrastructure projects, within a statutory time limit. Applications are submitted to and examined by the IPC in a prescribed process. Each of the prescribed stages addresses rights, responsibilities and a time-frame for applicants, the IPC and other interested parties to the application.

The Planning Act makes it a statutory requirement for developers to consult local stakeholders before submitting the application to the IPC in the so-called pre-application phase. This ensures the inclusion of relevant responses into the consultation report to be submitted to the IPC as part of an application. The time-related process starts on receipt of any application by the IPC, where the IPC has to decide within 28 days whether the application will be accepted or not. During this phase, the IPC examines the adequacy of public consultation, whether the right environmental issues have been identified and whether the required amount and standard of information has been provided.

If an application is accepted, it will move to the pre-examination stage. The developer is then required to notify the relevant parties of the accepted application and publicise the proposal widely. During this stage, which takes at least another 28 days, the public will be able to register to put their case on the application. Only people who register as interested parties will be able to take part in the examination later on. All representations will be considered by the examining authority when receiving any application for a development consent order. Following the preliminary meeting and the agreed timetable for the local impact report and any hearings at the end of the pre-examination stage, the six-month examination phase starts, with further analysis of detailed views brought in by the registered stakeholders and a local impact report to be produced by the local authority.

On the basis of the information provided during the process, the IPC takes the decision on the application. However, under the Localism Act 2011, from 1 April 2012 the IPC has been abolished and its decision-making functions transferred to the Secretary of State, with examination of applications being carried out by the National Infrastructure Directorate of the Planning Inspectorate (PINS). This means that PINS will report to the Secretary of State with a recommendation. The Secretary of State has three months from receipt of the recommendation to make a development consent order (which may include conditions similar to those imposed on planning permissions) or refuse consent. A legal challenge must be taken up within six weeks after the development consent order has been made.

CRITIQUE

The United Kingdom faces significant challenges that are specific to its energy situation. These include:

- decline in domestic production of oil and natural gas;

- replacement of a fifth of power generating capacity by 2020;

- transition to a low-carbon economy and deployment of low-carbon technologies to meet ambitious targets.

Since the last IEA in-depth energy policy review in 2006, the United Kingdom has defined a strategy to move to a low-carbon economy and to tackle climate change with a remarkable sense of coherence, commitment and communication. Climate change is a priority. The government has clearly indicated its intent to deploy three low-carbon technology pathways: renewables, nuclear and carbon capture and storage (CCS).

Created in 2008, the Department of Energy and Climate Change (DECC) is responsible for mobilising synergies between energy and climate change policies. Part of the strategy includes ambitious legislative and operational frameworks including: the Climate Change Act, carbon budgets and a Carbon Plan, which is a government-wide plan of action on climate change. Specific institutions have been created to design, implement and evaluate policy actions, including DECC and the Committee on Climate Change. The institutional landscape seems rational and mobilises synergies. DECC staff deserve to be commended for their commitment to both energy and climate change issues.

The government demonstrates a high level of willingness to take action even though there currently is no long-term price signal for carbon that can influence financial and capital investment decisions. It has also been willing to propose new market-based regulations that are adapted to a changing context where security of supply and transition to a low-carbon energy future play a major role.

ENERGY MARKET REFORM

The government has been a leader in the liberalisation of energy markets. It recognised the need to identify and create structures that support competitive development of the electricity sector using open markets with clear price signals, high levels of liquidity and stable settings to attract timely and efficient investment.

The government has set challenging carbon emissions reduction targets that require a substantial transformation of its energy sector. Existing market settings appear unlikely to deliver the desired outcomes of security of supply, low-carbon emissions and affordability within the required time-frames. The proposed Electricity Market Reform (EMR) mechanisms present some major issues for the United Kingdom and probably also for the EU electricity market.

However, in response to market constraints, such as the lack of a long-term carbon price under the EU-ETS, there is now a need to deploy interventions that are transitional, applied only to the extent that the electricity security and decarbonisation goals would otherwise not be achieved in a timely manner. The proposed Electricity Market Reform is a very complex and challenging set of proposals that is intended to secure long-term electricity supply and decarbonise electricity generation, while minimising costs to the customer.

PUBLIC AWARENESS

A notable investment in communication and consultation has helped to develop a strong level of support throughout the political spectrum and among most stakeholders. Coherence in how the main stakeholders address climate change and energy transition as a central challenge is impressive: it is the fruitful result of the systematic process of consultation, communication and explanation, underpinned with comprehensive documentation.

While general awareness of energy and climate change issues has increased in the last five years and the take-up of domestic microgeneration technologies is more widespread, energy reducing behaviours among consumers are not yet mainstream. Trust in energy suppliers and institutions remains at a low level because of service and marketing issues, and price increases. From 2012 to 2015, more work will need to be done to re-establish trust in energy markets, drive demand for Green Deal energy efficiency measures and encourage active engagement with smart meters.

ENERGY TECHNOLOGY

Energy policy in the United Kingdom in the last two decades has focused on competitiveness. It now has to also focus on innovation and draw on broader technology choices. In the next decade, it is expected that about GBP 200 billion will be invested in energy infrastructure. This is a tremendous challenge in terms of industrial, financial and human resources. Power shortages could jeopardise not only the market reforms but also its social acceptance. Therefore, all stakeholders, including DECC, should work to develop consensus on an innovation and industrial development strategy which defines and sets out operational low-carbon technology roadmaps in a collaborative effort with industry.

INFRASTRUCTURE PLANNING

The Infrastructure Planning Commission (IPC) regime only covers England and Wales (with only limited exceptions for major infrastructure applications in Scotland). In some projects that include Scotland, therefore, two different planning processes may be involved, particularly where some of the project does not require consent under the Planning Act in its own right (*e.g.* electricity substations attached to a transmission project). This can lead to additional transaction costs and increased uncertainty in an already complex, detailed and long process. The government is encouraged to consider ways for harmonising planning procedures across Great Britain.

RECOMMENDATIONS

The government of the United Kingdom should:

☐ *Strengthen the co-ordinating role of DECC in its action on climate change and energy across the government, including the Department of Transport (biofuels, electric vehicles) and the Department for Business, Innovation and Skills (green growth) and the Treasury.*

☐ *Consider how to empower local governments and communities more effectively to find innovative solutions to local-level energy challenges, including networks and energy efficiency services.*

☐ *Increase public awareness of energy matters and raise consumer confidence in energy markets, particularly in light of pending reforms, e.g. the electricity market reform and the Green Deal, and of the need to invest in and pay for low-carbon capacity and energy.*

☐ *Define a clear industrial policy strategy for innovation and green growth with priorities and roadmaps for each low-carbon technology.*

☐ *Develop, together with industry and academia, a common vision and collaborative strategy to ensure that needs in human resources for the energy sector are met.*

☐ *Ensure flexibility through the major infrastructure planning and permitting process in order to have the ability to adapt applications and ensure timely planning consent.*

☐ *Consider ways to harmonise planning procedures between England, Wales and Scotland.*

3. CLIMATE CHANGE

Key data (2010)

Total greenhouse gas emissions (including LULUCF): 590 Mt of CO_2-equivalent, down 23% from 1990

2008-2012 target: -12.5% from base year

CO_2 emissions from fuel combustion: 484 Mt, down 12% from 1990

Emissions by fuel: natural gas 40%, oil 35%, coal 25%

Emissions by sector: electricity and heat generation 38%, transport 25%, households 17%, industry 10%, other 10%

OVERVIEW

The United Kingdom is a signatory to the United Nations Framework Convention on Climate Change (UNFCCC) and a party to the Kyoto Protocol. Strong action to mitigate climate change both at home and abroad enjoys broad political support.

The United Kingdom has a target to reduce its greenhouse gas (GHG) emissions to an average of 12.5% below their base year[1] in the period 2008-2012, in absolute terms from 780 Mt CO_2-eq to 683 Mt CO_2-eq. According to DECC, total GHG emissions in 2010, including land use, land-use change and forestry (LULUCF), amounted to 590.4 Mt CO_2-eq, which is 24.3% less than in the base year, but 3.1% more than in 2009. In 2010, carbon dioxide (CO_2) accounted for 84.6% of GHGs, methane (CH_4) for 7.0%, nitrous oxides (N_2O) for 5.9% and the F-gases (hydrofluorocarbons, perfluorocarbons and sulphur hexafluoride) for 2.6%.

Beyond 2012, as part of the effort-sharing of the EU GHG target of -20% from 1990 to 2020, the United Kingdom will have to limit GHG emissions to 16% below their 2005 levels in the sectors outside the EU Emissions Trading Scheme (ETS). The ETS sector has a single EU-wide target of -21% from 2005 to 2020. The UK's official policy is to increase the EU emissions reduction target for 1990 to 2020 from 20% to 30%

The United Kingdom has ambitious national targets beyond 2020, as laid out in the 2008 Climate Change Act. The Act introduces a binding long-term framework to reduce greenhouse gas emissions, towards a long-term target of at least an 80% reduction below 1990 levels by 2050. A system of "Carbon Budgets", which limit UK emissions over successive five-year periods, will set the trajectory to 2050. Carbon Budgets have now been adopted up to 2027 by which year carbon emissions must be halved from the 1990 levels.

---

1. Kyoto base year consists of emissions of carbon dioxide CO_2, methane CH_4 and nitrous oxide N_2O in 1990, and of hydrofluorocarbons, perfluorocarbons and sulphur hexafluoride SF6 in 1995. Includes an allowance for net emissions from LULUCF in 1990.

ENERGY-RELATED CO$_2$ EMISSIONS

SOURCES OF CO$_2$ EMISSIONS

In 2010, carbon dioxide (CO$_2$) emissions from fossil fuel combustion represented 97% of total CO$_2$ emissions and around 82% of greenhouse gas (GHG) emissions in the United Kingdom. CO$_2$ emissions from fuel combustion totalled 510 million tonnes (Mt) in 2008, a level that had been relatively stable in the previous few years. With the economic downturn, CO$_2$ emissions fell by 9% in 2009 to 466 Mt, the lowest level since 1973, and in 2010 emissions increased to 484 Mt.[2]

The drop in CO$_2$ emissions in 2009 was largely from lower levels of coal- and natural gas-fired combustion. While CO$_2$ emissions were lower in 2009 in all sectors, they fell by 15% in industry and by 11% in power and heat generation from 2008. From 2009 to 2010, CO$_2$ emissions from energy use increased by around 4.5%, which primarily resulted from a rise in residential gas use, combined with fuel switching away from nuclear power to coal and gas for electricity generation.

Since 1990, CO$_2$ emissions from the energy supply sector have decreased by 15% and business emissions by 41%, according to IEA data. However, emissions from households have increased by 8% and from road transport by 4%. Emissions reductions are primarily explained by switching from coal and oil to natural gas in power generation in the 1990s, reductions in energy-intensive industry output and improvements in energy efficiency.

Figure 7. **CO$_2$ emissions by sector*, 1973 to 2010**

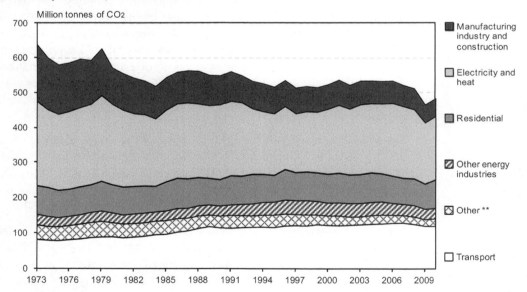

* Estimated using the IPCC Sectoral Approach.

** *Other* includes emissions from commercial, public services, agriculture/forestry and fishing sectors.

Source: *CO$_2$ Emissions from Fuel Combustion*, IEA/OECD Paris, 2011.

---

2. The analysis in this section is based on estimates done by the IEA by using the Intergovernmental Panel on Climate Change's default methods and emission factors.

Figure 7 shows CO_2 emissions by sector for 1973 to 2010. CO_2 emissions from natural gas combustion were responsible for 40% of the total in 2010 compared with an average for IEA countries of 24%. Oil combustion accounted for 35% of total CO_2 emissions. The United Kingdom, along with the Netherlands and Hungary, are the only three IEA countries where CO_2 emissions from natural gas combustion are higher than those from oil or coal. The power and heat generation sector is the largest emitter in the United Kingdom, responsible for 182 Mt of CO_2 in 2010. The transport sector accounts for 25% of total CO_2 emissions equal to 119 Mt. CO_2 emissions from other sectors are lower: residential at 81 Mt; industry at 50 Mt and other at 52 Mt.

CARBON INTENSITY

The United Kingdom emitted 0.27 tonnes of CO_2 per USD 1 000 of gross domestic product (GDP) on a purchasing power parity (PPP) basis in 2009 (Figure 8). This is nearly 30% lower than the IEA average and the seventh-lowest value among IEA member countries. Since 2000, the United Kingdom has reduced the carbon intensity of its economy by almost 22%. This is much faster than the IEA average of 17%.

Carbon intensity in power and heat generation has decreased considerably over the past two decades. In 2009, average emissions from power and heat generation were 450 g CO_2 per kilowatt-hour (kWh) in the United Kingdom, one-third lower than in 1990, and close to the OECD average of 420 g CO_2 per kWh. Government policy is to drive this carbon intensity significantly lower in the coming decades by promoting renewable sources, nuclear power and CCS (see Chapters 8 and 10).

Figure 8. Energy-related CO_2 emissions per GDP in the United Kingdom and in selected IEA countries, 1973 to 2009

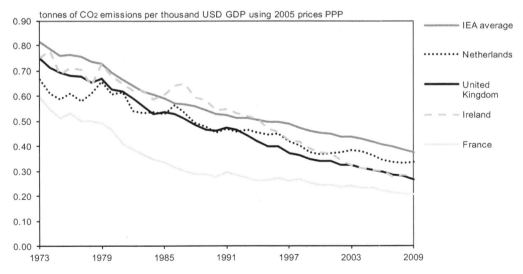

Sources: *Energy Balances of OECD Countries*, IEA/OECD Paris, 2011; *National Accounts of OECD Countries*, OECD Paris, 2011.

INSTITUTIONS

The **Department of Energy and Climate Change** (DECC), created in 2008 by merging energy policy and climate change policy into one department, has overall responsibility for the government's climate change mitigation policy. The **Department for Environment, Food and Rural Affairs** (DEFRA) has responsibility for climate change adaptation. Other government departments have responsibility for delivering specific policies and measures designed to deliver the United Kingdom's 2050 emissions reduction target. These include the **Department for Transport, the Department for Communities and Local Government**, the **Department for Business, Innovation and Skills,** and the **Treasury**.

The 2008 Climate Change Act set up an independent body, the Committee on Climate Change, with statutory responsibilities to propose appropriate carbon budgets, assess progress towards the government's long-term emissions reduction targets and give advice to the government on climate change policies in general, covering both mitigation of and adaptation to climate change.

POLICIES AND MEASURES

OVERVIEW

The United Kingdom has a unilateral legally binding target to reduce greenhouse gas emissions by at least 80% of 1990 levels by 2050. The target was set as part of the 2008 Climate Change Act. The 2050 target is to be delivered through Carbon Budgets which limit UK emissions over successive five-year periods. The Act also set up an expert body, the Committee on Climate Change, to advise the government.

A medium-term target of a 34% reduction by 2020 was also adopted, with the promise of a further tightening in the event of a global deal on climate change. To achieve this target, the Act established the principle of five-year Carbon Budgets. The first three Carbon Budgets were set in law in May 2009 and require reductions of 22% (2008-2012), 28% (2013-2017) and 34% (2018-2022) below 1990 levels. These targets are in line with the United Kingdom's share of the EU's 2020 commitments.

In July 2009, the government published the Low Carbon Transition Plan, the long-term strategy to deliver the targets, which set out policies and proposals to meet the first three Carbon Budgets. The fourth Carbon Budget (covering 2023-2027) was set in law of June 2011, requiring reductions of 50% from 1990, or 1 950 Mt CO_2 equivalent. In December 2011, the government published the Carbon Plan, which sets out specific milestones in each sector of the economy, department by department, which will deliver the Carbon Budget targets. DECC prepared extensive scenario analysis to support the Carbon Plan (2050 Pathways). Some of the key measures in the Carbon Plan affecting business and industry are outlined in the following sections.

EU EMISSIONS TRADING SCHEME (EU-ETS)

The EU-ETS established in 2003 by Directive 2003/87/EC is a mandatory cap-and-trade system covering CO_2 emissions from installations in nine energy-intensive sectors: combustion installations (power and heat generation), refinery processes, coke ovens, metal ores, steel, cement, glass, ceramics, and cellulose and paper. The EU-ETS was launched in 2005 and its first commitment period ran until the end of 2007. The second phase covers 2008-2012. Installations in the EU-ETS can meet their obligations either by implementing emissions reduction measures of their own, or by purchasing allowances from other installations covered by the EU-ETS, or by purchasing credits from the Kyoto Protocol's flexible mechanisms (Joint Implementation or the Clean Development Mechanism).

According to the United Kingdom's National Allocation Plan for the second phase of the EU-ETS (2008-2012), the country's total annual allocation was to be about 246 million allowances per year. This figure includes 219 million allowances for activities that were covered by Phase I (2005-2007), 9.6 million allowances to cover emissions from expansion of scope in Phase II and around 17 million to be auctioned or sold in Phase III (2013-2020). The United Kingdom intends to auction around 7% of its allowances, some 85 million allowances, plus any surplus from the New Entrants Reserve.

Large electricity producers were allocated the most allowances, 107 million per year. Both combined heat and power (CHP) producers and iron and steel producers received more than 24 million and offshore installations (oil and gas) received 20 million. Other sectors were allocated far less on average.

Allowances to process industries were allocated for free on the basis of their past performance and business-as-usual, while benchmarking was applied to the allocation to large electricity producers (LEPs).

From 2013, new rules for the EU-ETS will apply. For example, all allowances for the power sector will have to be auctioned, whereas the manufacturing industry will still receive part of its allowances for free, on the basis of stringent EU-wide benchmarks. Trade-exposed energy-intensive sectors will receive 100% of the benchmark value, while other industrial sectors will receive 80% of the benchmark, phasing out to 30% in 2020.

DECC expects the EU-ETS to cover around half (48%) of national CO_2 emissions in the 2013-2020 period (Phase III) and expects the EU-ETS to deliver around two-thirds of emissions reductions in the first three Carbon Budgets.

DOMESTIC MEASURES OUTSIDE THE EU-ETS

Over the past decade, the United Kingdom adopted several carbon-related policy instruments:

The Climate Change Levy (CCL) and the Climate Change Agreements (CCAs)

Introduced in 2001, the CCL is a tax on energy for lighting, heating and power supplied to businesses and the public sector. Revenue from the levy is fed back to businesses through a 0.3% reduction in their national insurance contributions. From 1 April 2011 the CCL is GBP 4.85 per MWh for electricity, GBP 1.69 per MWh for natural gas and GBP 13.21 per tonne for coal. The CCAs are voluntary agreements for energy-intensive companies and offer up to an 80% discount on the CCL, if the companies meet targets on energy efficiency or emissions reduction. Renewable electricity suppliers are exempt from the CCL.

Carbon Emissions Reduction Target (CERT)

Established in 2008, CERT follows on from the Energy Efficiency Commitment (EEC). It obliges large energy suppliers to help households reduce their carbon emissions. The companies meet this obligation mainly through the promotion (typically free and subsidised offers) of insulation, lighting and other energy efficiency measures. Compared to EEC, CERT puts a greater focus on more substantial and robust household energy-saving measures such as insulation, and a component targeted on those most vulnerable to fuel poverty. The total lifetime savings required from energy suppliers over the duration of the scheme until 2012 is 293 Mt CO_2.

Community Energy Saving Programme (CESP)

Established in 2009 to complement CERT, the scheme achieves aims of both carbon reduction and addressing fuel poverty by requiring energy suppliers to achieve 19.25 Mt CO_2 lifetime savings in the most deprived areas of England, Scotland and Wales, promoting area-based and whole-house approaches to energy efficiency improvements.

Carbon Reduction Commitment Energy Efficiency Scheme (CRC EES)

Established in 2010 under the 2008 Climate Change Act, the scheme covers emissions by firms and public bodies not already subject to the EU system or substantially covered by other agreements. It comprises reporting requirements and a carbon levy. There are also several policies to promote energy efficiency in residential buildings.

Table 1. **Projected carbon emissions reductions by sector, 2008 to 2027**

Reductions (in MtCO$_2$-eq)	2008-2012	2013-2017	2018-2022	2023-2027
Power	116.6	177.4	282.5	120-160
Residential	63.4	149.1	189.8	9.6-50.3
Commercial and public services	23.9	44.9	78.2	12.5-27.8
Industry	13	21.5	47.2	63.1-111.6
Transport	1.8	23.3	62.7	28-80.8
Agriculture and waste	0	2.1	14.9	16.9
Total	**218.7**	**418.3**	**675.3**	**130.1-413.4**

Note: emissions savings are from baseline scenario plus additional measures, except for period 2023-2027 which shows an estimated range.

Source: DECC: *The Carbon Plan, delivering our low carbon future.* Annex B. 2011.

Decarbonisation of the economy is supported also indirectly through policies to increase energy efficiency, renewable energy supply (including through the Renewables Obligation, Renewable Transport Fuel Obligation, Renewable Heat Incentive, feed-in tariffs), nuclear energy, electricity market reform and technology innovation. These policies and measures are detailed in Part II of this report.

The December 2011 Carbon Plan outlines the following four areas as having significant potential to help reduce emissions:

- decarbonising power generation;

- Insulating homes better to improve their energy efficiency;

- replacing inefficient heating systems with more efficient, sustainable ones; and

- ultra-low carbon vehicles, such as electric vehicles.

New measures will be supported financially by the Green Deal and the Green Investment Bank (see Chapter 4).

INTERNATIONAL MEASURES

Under the 2008 Climate Change Act, the government must set a limit in sectors outside the EU-ETS on the use of credits for each Carbon Budget period 18 months in advance. The United Kingdom has set a zero limit on the use of international carbon offset credits in the first Carbon Budget period (2008-2012). In June 2011, the government decided the limit will be 55 Mt for the second Carbon Budget period (2013-2017). Under the Act, the government is also required to take into account the advice of the Committee on Climate Change and to consult the Devolved Administrations before setting the limit.

CRITIQUE

The passage of the 2008 Climate Change Act by the government has made the United Kingdom a world leader in climate change response. The country's long-term goal is a minimum 80% reduction in emission levels by 2050. The government has committed to establishing legally binding five-year emissions budgets and on 30 June 2011 set in law its fourth Carbon Budget which sets the ambitious goal of a reduction in GHG emissions of 50% by 2027. The mechanism to set targets three periods in advance provides significant certainty. The Committee on Climate Change advises the government on a broad range of discussions among issues, and the committee's independence increases transparency and certainty.

To reach the identified targets, the United Kingdom has specific measures already in place, and through its detailed Carbon Plan is also looking to establish a number of new policies. These measures typically are targeting specific activities or sectors.

Various national policies are intended to address climate change, including the electricity market reform (EMR), the Green Investment Bank, the Green Deal (to promote energy efficiency for residential consumers), and the Climate Change Agreements (for energy-intensive industries linked to the Climate Change Levy). Given the complexity of the policy framework, there may be scope for simplification to reduce compliance costs and increase efficiency. In particular, a number of pricing policies (EU-ETS, carbon price floor, CCL, CCAs, CRC scheme) overlap and result in different effective carbon prices being seen in different parts of the economy. As energy price rises contribute to concerns around fuel poverty and industrial competitiveness, it is important that carbon pricing policies are designed and aligned to operate as efficiently as possible.

The United Kingdom negotiates internationally on climate change as part of the European Union. The government has demonstrated a strong commitment to the EU development of strong common positions in the negotiations. The United Kingdom is seeking to strengthen EU commitments, including a 30% emissions reduction target by 2020. The adoption of such an action would most likely lead to a higher carbon price across the EU. To complement its efforts both internationally and in the EU, the United Kingdom is also committed to strengthening its bilateral relationships in order to tackle climate change, most notably with major emerging economies, such as India and China. The IEA welcomes the United Kingdom's strong international commitments and encourages it to continue its efforts.

RECOMMENDATIONS

The government of the United Kingdom should:

☐ *Enhance communication and information to the general public, in particular maximise the use of 2050 pathways as an admirable way of communicating the range of possible choices; review the technology assumptions regularly, update them as needed and complement them by other information initiatives.*

☐ *Evaluate the need for the full range of existing and recently introduced policies; in particular, consider in what way they interact on each other in order to avoid duplication and redundancy, to improve efficiency and to reduce compliance costs.*

☐ *Continue to play a strong role in international climate change negotiations; maintain its active role in the European Union, particularly when it comes to strengthening the EU-ETS in order to arrive at a more robust EU-wide carbon price.*

4. ENERGY EFFICIENCY

Key data (2010)

Total final consumption: 138 Mtoe (oil 41%, natural gas 34%, electricity 20%, biofuels and waste 2%, coal 2%, heat 1%), -7.9% since 2000

Consumption by sector: transport sector 32%, residential 30%, industry 25%, services and agriculture 13% (IEA average in 2009: transport 32%, residential 20%, industry 31%, services and agriculture 16%)

FINAL ENERGY USE

Total final energy consumption (TFC) in the United Kingdom was 138 million tonnes of oil equivalent (Mtoe) in 2010, up 5% from the previous year, 7.2% lower than in 2005 and around the same level as in 1990. Lower levels of energy consumption in recent years have mainly been in the industry sector where it fell by 19% and in commercial buildings with a decline of 9% between 2005 and 2010. Energy consumption in transport has decreased by only 3% since 2005 but it increased in residential buildings by 2% over the same period.

In fact, the residential sector was the largest energy-consumer in the United Kingdom in 2010. It consumed 45 Mtoe, nearly a third of TFC. This share is among the highest in IEA countries, where the average residential sector share in TFC is 20%. Transport is the second-largest, accounting for 30% of TFC. Industry accounted for 25% of final energy consumption in 2010, and commercial and other sectors consumed 13%.

Since 2005, the amount of natural gas in TFC has decreased by 7%, oil by 11% and electricity by 6%. Renewable sources, in turn, have seen their amount increase almost threefold to account for 2% of TFC.

The government forecasts TFC to decrease from 2010 to 2020. Biofuels and waste are the fuel source that is expected to grow the most significantly to reach nearly 8% of TFC in 2020.

INSTITUTIONS

The **Department of Energy and Climate Change** (DECC) has lead responsibility for energy efficiency policy. Within DECC, the work is delegated to the **Energy Efficiency Deployment Office**, established in February 2012.

However, there are some areas where other departments have a key interest or hold responsibility for a specific issue. For example, while DECC has responsibility for policy on the energy efficiency of existing buildings and homes, the **Department for Communities and Local Government** is responsible for minimum energy performance requirements for new buildings and homes. Responsibility for ecodesign and labelling of energy-using products lies with the **Department for Environment, Food and Rural Affairs**.

Figure 9. **Total final consumption by sector and by source, 1973 to 2020**

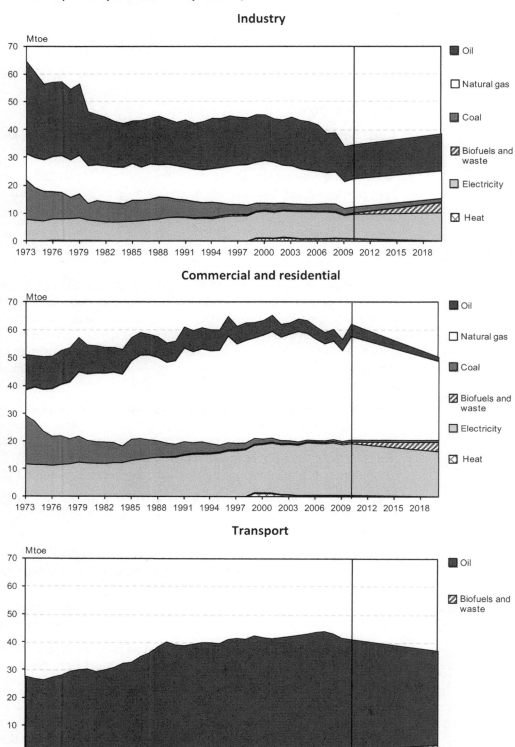

Sources: *Energy Balances of OECD Countries*, IEA/OECD, Paris, 2011 and country submission.

In terms of human resources, DECC has about 65 full-time equivalents working on energy efficiency policy for homes and businesses. This does not include work on the roll-out of smart meters or policy on microgeneration technologies.

Responsibility for the administration of the government's key household energy efficiency schemes, including the Carbon Emissions Reduction Target, resides with the **Office of Gas and Electricity Markets** (Ofgem), the energy sector regulator.

POLICIES AND MEASURES

The United Kingdom's various policies and measures to improve energy efficiency and save energy originate at both EU and national levels. EU regulations are directly applicable in all member states, while EU directives leave the member countries room to decide how to implement them. The national measures are typically aimed at reducing carbon emissions.

EUROPEAN UNION POLICIES

The United Kingdom's energy efficiency policies are guided by several EU regulations and directives. The Directive on Energy End-Use Efficiency and Energy Services (2006/32/EC) seeks to encourage energy efficiency through the development of a market for energy services and the delivery of energy efficiency programmes and measures to end-users. The directive requires member states to create national energy efficiency action plans and to meet an indicative target to reduce final energy use in the sectors outside the EU-ETS by 9% from the early 2000s to 2016. The EU has also adopted a non-binding target for 2020 to reduce primary energy use in the Union by 20% from baseline projections. The directive also sets the framework for measures such as financing, metering, billing, promotion of energy services, and obligations for the public sector. In addition, it requires member states to oblige energy distributors or retailers to offer either competitively priced energy services, audits or other measures to improve energy efficiency.

The Directive on the Energy Performance of Buildings (EPBD, 2002/91/EC) sets requirements for energy efficiency in building codes, including minimum energy performance requirements (MEPs) and energy certificates. A recast of the EPBD (2010/31/EU) was adopted in May 2010 to strengthen the energy performance requirements and to clarify and streamline some provisions.

The recast Directive Establishing a Framework for Setting Ecodesign Requirements for Energy-related Products (Ecodesign, 2009/125/EC) aims to improve energy efficiency throughout a product's life cycle. It applies to products that use energy and to products that have an impact on energy use, such as building components. Product-specific standards will be set by EU regulations based on the directive.

Requirements for energy labelling of household appliances are based on several directives adopted over the past two decades. The recast of the Energy Labelling Directive (2010/30/EU) expands the mandatory labelling requirement to cover commercial and industrial appliances and also energy-related appliances; product-specific labelling standards are set up under this directive.

Recent EU transport policies aim to reduce CO_2 emissions from new passenger cars. In May 2009, the EU adopted Regulation 443/2009 to reduce CO_2 emissions from new passenger cars to reach a fleet average of 130 grams (g) CO_2 per kilometre by 2015. From 2020 on, this limit will be 95 g CO_2 per km. The regulation will be complemented by measures to further cut emissions by 10 g CO_2 per km. Complementary measures include efficiency improvements for car components with the highest impact on fuel consumption, and a gradual reduction in the carbon content of road transport fuels. A similar type of regulation for new vans was adopted in May 2011 (Regulation 510/2011).

Table 2. Key policies and expected carbon savings

Energy efficiency improvement programmes, energy services, and other measures to improve energy efficiency planned for achieving the target	Annual energy savings expected by end 2010		Annual energy savings expected by end 2016		Annual energy savings expected by end 2020	
	TWh	MtCO$_2$-eq	TWh	MtCO$_2$-eq	TWh	MtCO$_2$-eq
Household sector	**58.5**	**14.9**	**125.6**	**31.6**	**154.0**	**39.1**
Building regulations	22.4	4.3	40.9	7.8	48.8	9.4
Supplier obligations	26.7	7.6	61.4	14.8	66.1	15.9
Products policy	1.4	0.7	8.5	3.8	18.8	5.7
In-home displays/smart meters	0	0	5.0	1.3	8.5	2.2
Renewable Heat Incentive	0	0	1.3	1.2	3.3	3.3
Warm Front (fuel poverty measure)	8.0	2.4	8.4	2.6	8.4	2.6
Private and public sectors	**17.1**	**4.7**	**36.4**	**13.0**	**47.5**	**25.7**
Building regulations (2010 Part L)	0	0	4.3	1.2	5.6	1.5
Building regulations (2002+2005)	8.3	1.9	6.9	1.4	6.1	1.3
Business smart metering	0	0	2.8	0.6	4.9	1.1
Climate Change Agreements	7.5	2.1	7.5	2.1	7.5	2.1
CRC Energy Efficiency Scheme	0.1	0	3.8	0.7	7.7	1.5
Energy Performance of Buildings Directive	0	0	0.9	0.3	1.6	0.5
Products policy	1.6	0.7	6.0	2.6	10.3	4.4
Renewable Heat Incentive	0	0	-1.5	4.0	-1.9	13.3
Energy-intensive industry	0	0	5.7	0	5.7	0
Transport	**17.3**	**8.2**	**37.4**	**19.4**	**60.6**	**30.4**
EU voluntary agreement to 2009	16.6	5.1	24.7	7.6	25.0	7.7
Interim EU target to 130 g CO$_2$/kg	0	0	4.9	1.5	13.1	4.0
Biofuels in transport	0	2.9	0	7.9	0	11.6
Low-carbon buses & SAFED bus driver training	0.4	0.1	0.8	0.3	1.1	0.4
EU new car CO$_2$ regulation: 95 g CO$_2$/km target for 2020	0	0	0.9	0.3	12.0	3.7
Low Carbon Transition Plan additional intended measures	0.4	0.1	6.1	1.9	9.4	3.0
Total energy and carbon savings*	**93.3**	**27.8**	**199.4**	**63.9**	**262.1**	**95.1**

* This includes only quantified policies. Notable exceptions include savings from tax policy, such as the Climate Change Levy and the Enhanced Capital Allowances.

Source: DECC: UK Report on Articles 4 and 14 of the EU End-use Efficiency and Energy Services Directive (ESD), July 2011. The figures for smart meters and the CRC Energy Efficiency Scheme were revised in March 2012.

NATIONAL POLICIES

Policies and measures in the United Kingdom are listed in the 2007 National Energy Efficiency Action Plan (NEEAP) and its 2011 revision as well as in the 2011 Carbon Plan. Actions in major sectors are outlined in Table 2 and the sectoral sections below. Several carbon-related policy instruments help to improve energy efficiency. They are listed in Chapter 3.

BUILDINGS

The United Kingdom has one of the oldest building stocks in Europe and its turnover rate is rather slow. According to DECC, houses built before 2009 are expected to account for two-thirds of the UK housing stock in 2050. The Energy Saving Trust, in turn, puts this share at around three-quarters.

The average new home built in England requires about half as much energy per square metre as the average existing home. UK building regulations were revised and strengthened in 2010 and additional revisions will follow in 2013 and 2016, so that by 2016, all new build dwellings will be to a zero-carbon standard. There are plans for these requirements to be extended to non-residential buildings by 2019.

Insulation is the focus area of energy efficiency in buildings. According to DECC, in 2009 space heating accounted for 62% of final energy consumption in the domestic sector and 43% in the services sector. Building regulations require new homes to reach thermal efficiency standards which would typically be met by insulating lofts and cavity walls. Existing homes have been retrofitted through government schemes or through a do-it-yourself loft insulation. As a result of new build and retrofitting insulation, the number of homes with cavity wall insulation increased by 27% from April 2007 to April 2011, such that 10.8 million of the 18.7 million homes with cavities are insulated. The number of homes with loft insulation of at least 125 mm-thick increased by 39% from April 2007 to April 2011, such that 13.2 million of the 23.3 million homes with lofts are insulated.

The Green Deal and Energy Company Obligation (ECO) will be the government programmes for tackling the insulation challenge (see Box 1). The government is establishing the Green Deal framework to enable private firms to offer consumers energy efficiency improvements to their homes, community spaces and businesses at no up-front cost, and recoup payments through a charge in instalments on the energy bill.

The Energy Act 2011 introduced powers alongside the Green Deal to require private landlords, as from 2016, to make reasonable energy efficiency improvements requested by tenants, and by 2018 to improve the least efficient properties ensuring they are brought up to a minimum energy efficiency rating of 'E' before they can be rented out, or have carried out the maximum package of measures under the Green Deal and the Energy Company Obligation (ECO), provided there are no net negative costs to landlords.

Energy performance certificates (EPCs) are required of a sale, rent or construction of a building. The EPC scheme, an obligation under EU Directive 2006/32/EC, is fully rolled out and includes an A to G rating of the buildings performance together with recommendations for cost-effective action to improve building efficiency and links to sources of advice.

The government's fuel poverty policies contain several energy efficiency dimensions. The Warm Front scheme in England provides eligible low-income households occupying low-efficiency homes with efficient heating systems, insulation, and draught proofing. Since its launch in June 2000, the scheme has assisted over 2.2 million households in England, with an average potential saving of over GBP 650 per year per household during the lifetime of the scheme.

Fuel poverty measures that help improve energy efficiency in buildings also include the Carbon Emissions Reduction Target and the Community Energy Savings Programme (see Chapter 3). These two measures are planned to be replaced by the ECO Affordable Warmth target. The target is intended to improve solid wall properties, which have not benefited much from previous schemes. As well as saving carbon, it is intended to improve the ability of the vulnerable and those on lower incomes to heat their homes affordably.

Box 1. **The Green Deal and the Energy Company Obligation**

The Green Deal is a market framework which will enable private firms in Great Britain to offer consumers energy efficiency improvements to their homes, community spaces or businesses at no up-front cost with repayments recouped through a charge made in instalments on their energy bill. The scheme was established through the Energy Act 2011, and the government expects the first Green Deals to be available from October 2012.

The Green Deal will operate alongside a new Energy Company Obligation (ECO). Millions of homes could benefit from heating and insulation measures and so would non-domestic properties.

A key element of Green Deal finance is that only packages of measures that pay for themselves over the lifetime of the Green Deal will qualify. It will allow households and businesses to enjoy the benefits of efficiency measures and the energy bill savings they can bring, without the need for up-front finance. If they move to a different property, the charge will not move with them, meaning that those in the property will pay from the savings they make.

The ECO will provide support for those properties that may be more expensive to treat and so need extra funding to pay back within the Green Deal finance period. ECO is also intended to help the poorest and most vulnerable households, who need improvements to the energy performance of their homes and for whom the Green Deal may not be accessible.

The success of the Green Deal will depend on the trust of consumers and businesses in the impartiality, quality and robustness of the advice and recommendations provided. The government is looking to provide support through a remote advice (web/phone-based) service.

Source: DECC: UK Report on Articles 4 and 14 of the EU End-use Efficiency and Energy Services Directive (ESD). July 2011.

INDUSTRY AND SERVICES

Energy efficiency improvements are encouraged by several carbon reduction instruments, such as the Climate Change Levy, the Climate Change Agreements and the Carbon Reduction Commitment Energy Efficiency Scheme and, in energy-intensive industry, the EU-ETS (see Chapter 3).

The Carbon Trust grants zero-interest loans for energy efficiency investments. It also manages the Enhanced Capital Allowance (ECA) scheme which encourages businesses to invest in energy-efficient equipment by enabling them to claim 100% first-year capital allowance on the purchase of qualifying energy-saving plant and machinery.

The Carbon Trust has produced a series of energy benchmarking tools, including for the industrial buildings sector. These encourage the implementation of comprehensive energy management procedures and practices and provide a comprehensive package of energy and carbon management advice and information for business and the public sector.

The government provides several types of incentives for the uptake of combined heat and power production. These include an exemption from the Climate Change Levy, eligibility for Energy Capital Allowances, eligibility for enhanced Renewables Obligation certificates for biomass CHP and reduced value-added tax on the installation of micro-CHP.

TRANSPORT

Private cars are by far the dominant form of travel in the United Kingdom (see Table 3). Traffic volume by private cars increased by 16% from 1990 to 2009, half the EU15 average. Bus use declined by one-fifth, while tram and metro use increased by half and railway use by 16% over the same period. Private cars and taxis alone accounted for 58% of all UK carbon emissions from domestic transport in 2009, while light vans made up a further 12.5%.

The United Kingdom today has over 8 million more registered passenger cars than in 1990, an increase of two-fifths. Car density has risen from 361 in 1990 to 470 per 1 000 residents in 2009, slightly less than the EU15 average of 503.

The transport of freight in the United Kingdom accounts for 22% of carbon emissions from domestic transport, according to government estimates. Freight is mostly transported by road which accounted for 86% of total tonne-kilometres in 2009, while rail accounted for 14%. Reflecting structural changes in the economy, freight volumes declined modestly from 1990 to 2009, while real GDP increased by close to 50%.

Table 3. **Modal split of passenger transport on land, 2009**

	Car	Bus	Train	Tram and metro
Share, %	87.1	4.9	6.8	1.2

Source: *EU Transport in Figures – Statistical Pocketbook 2011.*

Several measures have been adopted to improve more efficient energy use in transport. The efficiency of new vehicles will be improved through EU regulations. From 2015, new passenger cars sold in the EU may not emit more than 130 grams of CO_2 per kilometre. There is a further provisional longer-term target of 95 g CO_2 per km by 2020, representing a 40% reduction on 2007 levels. For new vans, these mandatory limits are 175 g CO_2 per km from 2017. A limit of 147 g CO_2 per km by 2020 has also been specified, representing a 28% reduction on 2007 levels.

The vehicle excise duty (VED) and company car tax, although primarily fiscal policy instruments, encourage the development and purchase of fuel-efficient vehicles in the United Kingdom, as their structure is based on CO_2 emissions.

For promoting ultra low emission vehicles (ULEVs), the government has a budget of more than GBP 400 million over the lifetime of the current Parliament (up to May 2015). This includes funding for a consumer incentive, infrastructure, and research and development.

The plug-In car grant commenced in January 2011 to help both private consumers and businesses purchase an electric, plug-in hybrid or hydrogen fuelled car. Buyers are able to receive a grant of 25% of the vehicle price, up to a value of GBP 5 000. In June 2011, the government published its *Infrastructure Strategy* for the development of recharging infrastructure in the United Kingdom. In support of this, around GBP 25 million will be provided through the Plugged-In Places programme to install charging infrastructure in eight cities around the country by March 2013.

The United Kingdom also has a voluntary labelling scheme for new car fuel economy which helps consumers to compare carbon emissions, fuel costs and vehicle tax for different cars. Over 90% of new car dealerships use the label. Following the success of this scheme, the United Kingdom's used car fuel economy label was launched in 2009 with support from dealerships, manufacturers, the Low Carbon Vehicle Partnership and the government. To date over quarter of a million labels have been circulated into the used car market and nearly 2 000 used car dealers have signed up to this voluntary scheme.

Eco-driving was introduced as part of driving licence tests in 2008. EU regulations to lower rolling resistance and maintain appropriate tyre inflation pressure through mandatory fitting of tyre-pressure monitoring systems will apply to all new cars from 2014.

Turning to other forms of transport, the government supports a progressive electrification of the rail network in England and Wales as a way of reducing the cost of running the railways, increasing passenger comfort and reducing carbon emissions. Currently, a third of the UK rail network is electrified. The government is also planning for the construction of high-speed rail lines linking London and Birmingham with Manchester and Leeds.

Low-carbon public transport is also being encouraged through the Green Bus Fund, where funding of almost GBP 47 million is expected to introduce around 550 new low-carbon buses across England. Low-carbon buses use at least 30% less fuel and emit nearly a third less carbon than a conventional bus.

Unnecessary travel can be reduced through wider use of information and communications technology. The government's objective is to have the best superfast broadband network in Europe by 2015. Broadband Delivery UK (BDUK), the government team delivering this agenda, has GBP 530 million of funding available to this end.

APPLIANCES

Requirements for minimum energy efficiency standards and energy labelling of appliances are based on EU law, in particular Directive 2009/125/EC and related product-specific regulations and Directive 2010/30/EU on energy labelling.

Smart meters

The government's vision is for every home and every small business in Great Britain to have smart electricity and gas meters. Smart meters are intended to deliver a range of benefits to consumers, energy suppliers and networks. Consumers will have real-time information on their energy consumption to help them control energy use, save money and reduce emissions. DECC estimates that smart metering will deliver GBP 7.1 billion net benefits to consumers, energy suppliers and networks for the period up to 2030. Domestic dual-fuel customers are expected to save on average GBP 22 per year by 2020 and GBP 42 by 2030. It is estimated that by 2020, the average small and medium non-domestic customer will save over GBP 100 per year on their energy bill as a result of having a smart meter. The roll-out will also support the development of a smart grid delivering improved network efficiency and responsiveness, and supporting the uptake of electric vehicles and microgeneration.

Smart meters are being installed in two phases; the Foundation Stage and mass roll-out. During the Foundation Stage, which began in April 2011, the government is working with industry, consumer groups and other stakeholders to ensure that all the necessary groundwork is completed for mass roll-out. The government expects the mass roll-out to start in 2014 and to be completed in 2019. The roll-out of smart meters will be undertaken by energy supply companies, and will involve replacing around 53 million gas and electricity meters in more than 30 million homes and businesses.

The transfer of data to and from household smart meters will be managed centrally by a new, GB-wide function covering both the electricity and gas sectors. This central Data and Communications Company (DCC) will be independent of suppliers and distributors.

PUBLIC AWARENESS

Natural gas and electricity prices rose rapidly in 2011 and become a political topic. In October 2011, the government, working with consumer groups, energy suppliers and Ofgem, agreed a range of measures to help consumers save gas and electricity, and therefore money. These measures were:

- Agreement on clear and transparent communications to make sure consumers know about the potential savings from checking on their energy deal, switching tariff and/or supplier, and insulating;

- A shared website and campaign material giving consumer advice (http://www.direct.gov.uk/en/Nl1/Newsroom/DG_199725);

- Customers seeking advice at the cheapest tariff will also be given advice on energy-saving measures, and vice versa;

- Ofgem and Citizens Advice announced record funding from suppliers for this year's Energy Best Deal campaign.

CRITIQUE

Energy efficiency is a central component of the UK energy policy and the country seeks to reduce its energy consumption by 9% from 2007 to 2016. Beyond that, improving energy efficiency will help meet the carbon budgets and the long-term goal of cutting carbon emissions by 80% from 1990 to 2050.

Ambitious minimum performance requirements (in terms of carbon emissions) for new buildings were introduced in 2010. Additional revisions will follow in 2013 and 2016 so that by 2016, all new-build dwellings will be zero-carbon. The IEA welcomes these improvements. The housing stock is growing at a rate of well below 1% per year and, according to DECC, around two-thirds of the building stock the United Kingdom will have in 2050 already exists. The government is therefore right to focus on the existing buildings.

Encouraging energy efficiency improvements in buildings is a complicated policy challenge in most countries. The Green Deal offers a new original way to respond to this challenge, as it will enable private firms to offer consumers energy efficiency improvements to homes, community spaces and businesses at no up-front cost, and recoup payments through a charge in instalments on the energy bill. The government is encouraged to define the details of the programme without delay so that it can be launched as planned in autumn 2012. It will also be important to establish clear guidelines for monitoring and evaluating progress.

The Green Deal will be primarily a financing tool. For it to be successful, the general public needs to be aware of the potential benefits it offers. Awareness-raising is particularly crucial, because the retrofitting work will largely be done by the private sector, potentially including utilities which do not enjoy the full confidence of the general public. The government should therefore continue and intensify efforts to raise awareness of the benefits of energy efficiency retrofits and pay particular attention to informing the public of how the Green Deal will work. The utilities in turn should try to better communicate that they have a legal obligation to reduce carbon emissions and for that reason, perhaps counter-intuitively, they are encouraging their customers to use less energy.

Smart meters will be essential for enabling more efficient use of gas and power. They will enable various operational savings to suppliers and wider energy service propositions to benefit consumers. Ultimately, they are also a key element in creating a smart grid. The government has well identified the key role of smart metering and has a plan to roll out over 50 million smart meters in the next few years. In order to fully realise the potential of regular information that smart meters will provide, the government should ensure that potential service providers can gain access to this information, subject to the customers' agreement and ensuring their privacy. Smart meters should also be robust and simple, and not create more barriers for new entrants, supplier switching, and other service providers (internet, home management).

Energy efficiency policies are framed as a key climate change response. However, they also have significant benefits in reducing electricity demand (and hence system costs), and therefore in reducing the need for additional generation to meet growth in demand. Energy efficiency measures targeted on slowing the growth in peak demand can also reduce the need for investments in distribution network. It is not clear whether the level of energy efficiency investment economy-wide is optimal for minimising costs across electricity generation and distribution sectors. There does not appear to be any mechanism to assess (and fund) the level of investment in energy efficiency that would be more cost-effective than equivalent new generation or grid investment. Similarly, the potential for demand-side response in contributing to peak load management (again both in terms of generation and distribution systems) could be developed further.

Also in the transport sector, energy efficiency is mainly promoted by the need to reduce GHG emissions, although it is also promoted indirectly through transport fuel taxes which are high by international comparison. The government is planning further emissions reductions by enhancing efficiency of all vehicles, reducing carbon intensity of fuels, promoting ultra low-emission vehicles (ULEVs) and investing in low-carbon infrastructure. Motoring taxes will have a key role in encouraging the development and purchase of ULEVs and supporting sustainable biofuels. The government's programme commits to mandating a national recharging network for electric and plug-in hybrid vehicles. In addition, the EU Fuel Quality Directive (2009/30/EC) introduces the requirement for fuel suppliers to reduce the life cycle greenhouse gas intensity of the fuel they supply by 6%˙ per unit of energy by 2020. All these policies should be commended. Considering that transport is the second-largest GHG-emitting sector, after energy supply, quick action should be taken to implement these measures. At the EU level, fuel efficiency standards have been developed for passenger cars and light commercial vehicles (vans). Following these positive examples, the IEA encourages the United Kingdom and other EU member states now to develop mandatory fuel efficiency standards also for heavy-duty vehicles.

Finally, the United Kingdom should continue its efforts to fully implement the IEA policy recommendations for improving energy efficiency (see Box 2).

Box 2. **IEA 25 energy efficiency policy recommendations**

To support governments with their implementation of energy efficiency, the IEA recommended the adoption of specific energy efficiency policy measures to the G8 summits in 2006, 2007 and 2008. The consolidated set of recommendations to these summits covers 25 fields of action across seven priority areas: cross-sectoral activity, buildings, appliances, lighting, transport, industry and power utilities. The fields of action are outlined below.

1. The IEA recommends action on *energy efficiency* across sectors. In particular, the IEA calls for action on:

- data collection and indicators;

- strategies and action plans;

- competitive energy markets, with appropriate regulation;

- private investment in energy efficiency; and

- monitoring, enforcement and evaluation.

2. *Buildings* account for about 40% of energy used in most countries. To save a significant portion of this energy, the IEA recommends action on:

- mandatory buildings codes and minimum energy performance requirements;

- net-zero energy consumption in buildings;

- improved energy efficiency in existing buildings; and

- building energy labels or certificates;

- energy performance of building components and systems.

3. *Appliances and equipment* represent one of the fastest growing energy loads in most countries. The IEA recommends action on:

- mandatory minimum energy performance standards and labels;

- test standards and measurement protocols; and

- market transformation policies.

Box 2. **IEA 25 energy efficiency policy recommendations** (continued)

4. Saving energy by adopting efficient *lighting technology* is very cost-effective. The IEA recommends action on:

- phase-out of inefficient lighting products; and

- energy-efficient lighting systems.

5. To achieve significant savings in the *transport sector,* the IEA recommends action on:

- mandatory vehicle fuel-efficiency standards;

- measures to improve vehicle fuel efficiency;

- fuel-efficiency non-engine components; and

- transport system efficiency.

6. In order to improve energy efficiency in *industry*, action is needed on:

- energy management;

- high-efficiency industrial equipment and systems;

- energy efficiency services for small and medium-sized enterprises; and

- complementary policies to support industrial energy efficiency.

7. *Energy utilities* can play an important role in promoting energy efficiency. Action is needed to promote:

- utility end-use energy efficiency schemes.

Implementation of IEA energy efficiency recommendations can lead to huge cost-effective energy and CO_2 savings. The IEA estimates that, if implemented globally without delay, the proposed actions could save around 7.6 Gt CO_2 per year by 2030. In 2010 this corresponded to 17% of annual worldwide energy consumption. Taken together, these measures set out an ambitious road-map for improving energy efficiency on a global scale.

RECOMMENDATIONS

The government of the United Kingdom should:

- ☐ *Define the details of the Green Deal as soon as possible to ensure timely implementation; raise public awareness of the benefits of the Green Deal; monitor and evaluate its implementation from early on.*

- ☐ *Continue efforts in energy efficiency improvement in the transport sector, paying particular attention to the overall cost-effectiveness of relevant policies and measures.*

- ☐ *Encourage the European Union to develop mandatory fuel efficiency standards for heavy-duty vehicles.*

- ☐ *Consider potential for increased investment in energy efficiency to lower electricity system costs for consumers, by reducing the growth rate of demand and hence the need for investment in additional generation and distribution infrastructure.*

PART II
SECTOR ANALYSIS

5. OIL AND NATURAL GAS

Key data (2010)

Oil

Production: 64.4 Mtoe (1.3 mb/d), down 51% from 2000

Share: 31% in total primary energy supply and 1% in electricity generation

Net imports: 11 Mtoe (0.2 mb/d)

Consumption: 63 Mtoe: transport 63%, industry 20%, energy sector 9%, households 5%, services and public 2%, electricity generation 2%.

Consumption per capita: 1 tonne per year, compared with IEA average of 1.7 tonnes per year.

Natural gas

Net production: 51.5 Mtoe (60 billion cubic metres), down 48% compared with 2000

Share: 42% in TPES and 46% in electricity generation

Net imports: 38% of supply, total imports 45.6 Mtoe (54 bcm); sources: Norway 48%, Qatar 27%, the Netherlands 15%, Belgium 4%, Trinidad and Tobago 3%, Algeria 2%, others 1%

Consumption: 85 Mtoe (99 bcm): power and heat generation 36%, residential 36%, industry 12%, commercial and public services 6%, energy sector 6%

OVERVIEW

With a combined oil and natural gas production of 117 million tonnes of oil equivalent (Mtoe) in 2010, the United Kingdom ranks fourth among the IEA countries and 17th worldwide (Table 4). Oil and gas production supports directly and indirectly around 350 000 jobs in the United Kingdom. It also brings significant revenue to the government, about GBP 10 billion in 2010/11.

All rights to the United Kingdom's hydrocarbon resources are vested in the Crown. Government policy strives to maximise economic production from domestic reserves, while taking into account environmental and safety concerns.

Almost all UK oil and gas is produced from offshore fields, mainly in the North Sea. The Petroleum Act of 1998 regulates the sector. As in all countries in the North Sea area, reserves and production are gradually declining (see Table 5 and Figures 4 and 11). Driven by higher oil prices, investment in oil and gas development has picked up in recent years.

Table 4. **Top 20 oil- and natural gas-producing countries, 2010**

Production (in Mtoe)		Oil	Gas	Total
1	Russian Federation	504	524	1 028
2	United States	373	559	932
3	Saudi Arabia	472	66	538
4	Iran	231	123	354
5	Canada	163	132	295
6	China	200	81	281
7	Mexico	155	38	194
8	Norway	101	91	192
9	Venezuela	159	21	180
10	Qatar	67	107	174
11	United Arab Emirates	131	43	174
12	Nigeria	136	23	159
13	Algeria	78	72	150
14	Kuwait	122	10	132
15	Indonesia	48	77	124
16	Brazil	110	13	122
17	United Kingdom	65	51	117
18	Iraq	115	1	116
19	Kazakhstan	81	24	105
20	Angola	93	1	94

Source: IEA.

Table 5. **Oil and natural gas reserve estimates, end 2010**

	Proven	Probable	Proven and probable	Possible	Maximum
Oil (million tonnes)					
Total oil reserves	374	282	656	222	878
Oil production, 2010	63				
Cumulative oil production to end 2010	3 446				
Estimated ultimate recovery	3 820	377	4 196	342	4 539
Natural Gas (billion cubic metres)					
Total natural gas reserves	253	267	520	261	781
Gas production, 2010	55				
Cumulative gas production to end 2010	2 337				
Estimated ultimate recovery	2 589	267	2 857	261	3 118

Source: Department of Energy and Climate Change.

Figure 10. **Oil and gas production on the UK continental shelf: income and expenditure, 1971 to 2008**

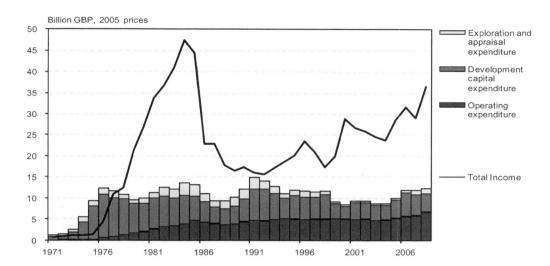

Source: Department of Energy and Climate Change.

PRODUCTION LICENSING

The government organises regular licensing rounds in order to encourage new exploration and production. The 26th offshore licensing round resulted in 144 licences being awarded to 83 companies in October 2010, as the first tranche, and another 46 licences being awarded to 32 companies in December 2011, as the second tranche. The 27th licensing round was launched in February 2012.

The United Kingdom has three main types of offshore production licences. They may cover three successive periods:

- Initial term: after which, if the agreed work programme has been completed and if a minimum amount of acreage has been relinquished, the licence may continue to a second term.

- Second term: after which, if a development plan has been approved and if all of the acreage outside that development has been relinquished, the licence may continue to a third term.

- Third term: which runs for an extended period to allow production.

The development of new oil and gas fields is authorised by the Secretary of State for Energy and Climate Change once the field development plan prepared by the licensee meets the government's requirements, the environmental impact assessment process has been completed successfully and the licensees have approved funding sufficient for their respective shares of the development costs.

Most of the 1 700 licences issued since the beginning of offshore hydrocarbon production have been traditional licences, *i.e.* Seaward Production Licences. These now have an initial term of four years, a second term of another four years and a third term of 18 years. An applicant must prove technical/environmental competence and financial capacity before being offered a traditional licence. The mandatory relinquishment at the end of the initial term is 50%.

Given the maturity of hydrocarbon production on the UK continental shelf, new types of licences have been introduced to maintain interest and investment: the Promote Licence and the Frontier Licence. The Promote Licence has been created to allow small companies to obtain a production licence first and attract the necessary operating and financial capacity later. Applicants need not prove technical/environmental competence or financial capacity before award, but they must do so within two years of the licence starting date in order to keep the licence, and they cannot operate until they have done so. During the first two years, the licence costs only a tenth of the traditional licence. Term durations and the mandatory relinquishment are the same as with a traditional licence.

The Frontier Licence comes in two forms related to the duration of the initial term: a six-year frontier licence and a nine-year frontier licence. These licences are designed to allow companies to evaluate large areas and the nine-year licence is specifically designed for exploration in the particularly harsh environment west of Scotland and west of Shetland. Both licences include a six-year second term and an 18-year third term. They also include a mandatory relinquishment of 75% after three years and an additional mandatory relinquishment of 50% of the remainder at the end of the initial term. As with the traditional licence, an applicant must prove technical/environmental competence and financial capacity before being offered a licence.

The licence for onshore production is a Petroleum Exploration and Development Licence (PEDL). It is similar in broad terms to the Seaward Production Licence, although for historical and practical reasons there are differences in the details:

- the initial term lasts for six years; the mandatory relinquishment at the end of the term is 50%;

- the second term lasts for five years;

- the third term lasts for 20 years.

Applicants must prove technical competence, awareness of environmental issues and financial capacity before being offered a PEDL.

UPSTREAM TAX REGIME

The tax regime that applies to oil and gas exploration and production in the United Kingdom and its continental shelf (UKCS) has three main elements:

Ring fence corporation tax is calculated in the same way as the standard corporation tax applicable to all companies, but with the addition of a "ring fence" and the availability of 100% first-year allowances for virtually all capital expenditure. The ring fence prevents taxable profits from oil and gas extraction from being reduced by losses from other activities or by excessive interest payments. Today's main rate of 30% tax on ring fence profits is set separately from the rate of mainstream corporation tax.

Supplementary charge is an additional charge on a company's ring fence profits (but with no deduction for finance costs). In March 2011, the rate of the supplementary charge was increased from 20% to 32%. The rationale for the increase was to fund a "fair fuel stabiliser" to reduce the fuel duty paid by motorists at a time of historically high oil prices in GBP terms.

Petroleum revenue tax **(PRT)** is a field-based tax charged on profits from oil and gas production from individual oilfields that were given development consent before 16 March 1993. The current rate of PRT is 50%. PRT is deductible as an expense in computing profits chargeable to ring fence corporation tax and supplementary charge.

The marginal tax rate is 81% on income from fields paying PRT, 30% on production income from qualifying new fields if that income is wholly covered by a "field allowance", otherwise it is 62%.

OIL SUPPLY AND DEMAND

PRODUCTION, IMPORTS AND EXPORTS

With oil production at 64.4 Mtoe (1.3 mb/d)[3] in 2010, the United Kingdom ranks fourth among the IEA countries, after the United States, Canada and Norway. UK oil production has declined on average by 7% per year since peaking at 143 Mtoe (2.9 mb/d) in 1999 (Figure 11). Since late 2005, the United Kingdom has been a net oil importer. The government expects production to continue to decrease and amount to about 41 Mtoe (0.8 mb/d) in 2020, some 40% less than today. In 2010, net imports accounted for 17% of total oil supply and on central projections this share is expected to rise to 48% in 2020.

Figure 11. **Indigenous oil production and net exports, 1973 to 2020**

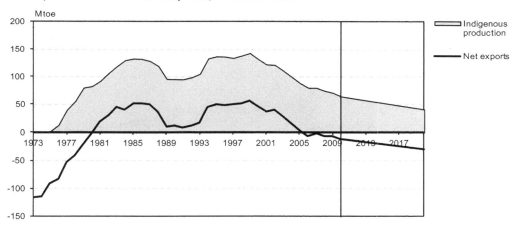

Sources: *Energy Balances of OECD Countries*, IEA/OECD Paris, 2011; country submission.

The United Kingdom exports two-thirds of its crude oil and natural gas liquids (NGL) production, mainly to the Netherlands (36% of total exports in 2010), the United States (18%), Germany (18%) and France (9%). In turn, it imports crude oil from Norway (32 Mtoe in 2010 or 68% of total imports), Russia (8%) and Libya (6%). The United Kingdom also exports one-third of its oil products, mainly to the Netherlands (21% of the total), the United States (20%), Ireland (14%) and France (6%).

---

3. The figure includes crude oil and NGL production.

DEMAND

Total oil consumption amounted to nearly 64 Mtoe in 2010, the same as in 2009 and 5% lower than in 2008. Over the last decade, oil demand has declined on average by 1% per year (Figure 12).

Transport is the largest oil-consuming sector in the United Kingdom. Its share of total oil consumption has increased from 56% in 2000 to 63% in 2010. Road transport accounted for 74% of total transport consumption, domestic and international aviation for 21% and the rest was consumed in rail transport and shipping. Reflecting the dominance of the transport sector oil consumption, the main oil products used are diesel, gasoline, and jet fuel and kerosene (Figure 13). Industry is the second-largest oil consumer, accounting for 20% of the total in 2010. This share has remained relatively constant over the last three decades. The energy sector consumed around 10% of the oil demand in 2010, households 5% and the commercial sector 1.7%.

Figure 12. **Oil supply by sector, 1973 to 2020***

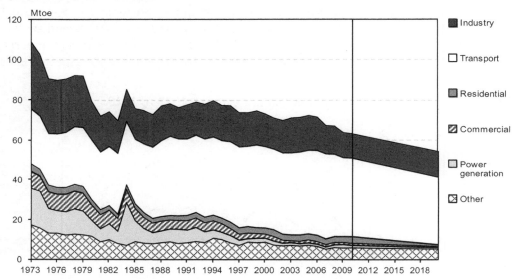

*Total primary energy supply by consuming sector. *Other* includes other transformation and energy sector consumption. *Industry* includes non-energy use. *Commercial* includes commercial, public services, agriculture/ forestry, fishing and other final consumption.

Sources: *Energy Balances of OECD Countries,* IEA/OECD Paris, 2011; and country submission.

Figure 13. **Oil consumption by product, 2010**

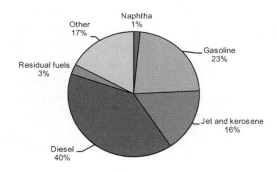

Source: *Oil Information*, IEA/OECD Paris, 2011.

OIL MARKET AND INFRASTRUCTURE

REFINERIES

Eight major refineries are operating in the United Kingdom, with a distillation capacity of around 88 Mtoe. The refineries are situated on the coast for ease of crude tanker access and together supply more than 90% of the inland market demand for oil products. There are also three small refineries (at Harwich, Eastham and Dundee) dedicated to speciality products, *e.g.* solvents, process oils and bitumen.

According to the UK Petroleum Industry Association, several challenges are facing the refining sector over the next ten years. These include weak refining margins; increasing global refining capacity and overcapacity; increasing environmental and regulatory burdens; lack of a level playing field with European refineries; and an increasing demand/supply imbalance of refined products.

Vertically integrated oil companies have traditionally dominated the refining sector, but in response to challenging domestic conditions and opportunities elsewhere, these international oil companies (IOCs) have reduced their presence in the domestic refining business. BP withdrew after the sale of its Grangemouth and Coryton refineries in 2007. In March 2011, Shell also exited after selling its Stanlow refinery to Essar Energy, and Chevron Texaco sold the Pembroke refinery and related downstream assets to Valero Energy Corporation.

Two other refineries are for sale (Total's Lindsey and Murco's Milford Haven facilities). In January 2011, Ineos announced a joint venture agreement with Petrochina for Grangemouth refinery and related assets. The current operators have not indicated any intention to convert these sites to import terminals or to stop refining activities in the event of a failure to sell the assets. Currently, Petroplus's filing for bankruptcy affects the Coryton refinery which it only recently acquired from BP.

STORAGE

Refineries contain the main storage facilities for crude and oil products in the United Kingdom and therefore represent major emergency oil reserve sites. Additionally, there are major product distribution terminals, which are self-contained, separate storage and distribution facilities, linked to refineries either by rail or pipeline. Altogether, these refinery and stand-alone terminals comprise a total of 59 primary distribution terminals. They are supplied by pipeline (51% of the volume), rail (15%) and sea (34%) from UK refineries. Some of them also receive finished products from abroad.

The terminals in turn supply products either directly to final consumers, such as individual petrol retail stations, or to commercial depots, which manage further distribution. The major distribution terminals usually handle large deliveries by tankers. Commercial depots receive smaller deliveries, such as those to depots owned by road haulage companies and used as central supply points for their fleets.

Figure 14. **Oil and natural gas infrastructure, 2010**

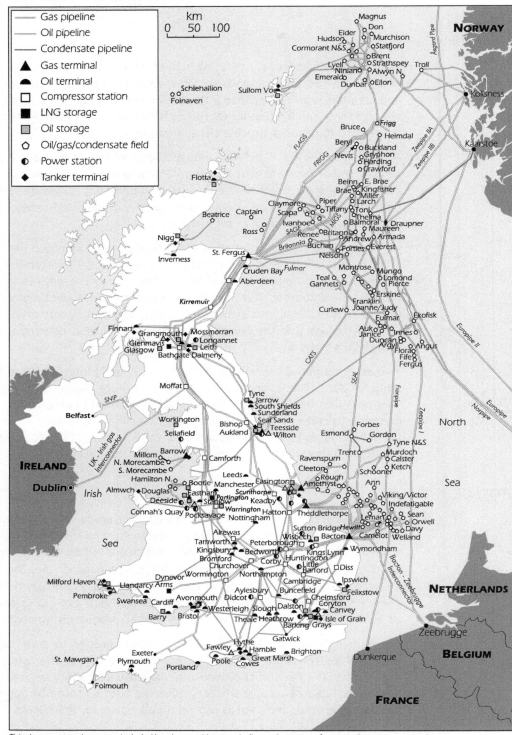

This document and any map included herein are without prejudice to the status of or sovereignty over any territory, to the delimitation of international frontiers and boundaries and to the name of any territory, city or area.

Source: IEA.

PIPELINES

The United Kingdom has a network of 4 800 km of private and government-owned oil pipelines (Figure 14). The pipelines are used both for short-distance transport, *e.g.* from jetty or import terminal to storage terminal or refinery, and over long distances to supply inland distribution terminals. Pipelines also connect the United Kingdom to offshore North Sea oil production (both from domestic and Norwegian fields).

The 2 400 km privately owned UK oil pipeline network carries a variety of oil products, from road transport fuels to heating oil and aviation fuel. It often comprises single pipelines that distribute several different products using batch flows, *e.g.* a volume of petrol being followed by a volume of gas/diesel oil. The network provides an efficient and robust distribution system across the United Kingdom and directly provides jet fuel for some of the major airports, including Heathrow, Gatwick, Manchester and Birmingham. The government also operates a separate oil pipeline system – the Government Pipeline and Storage System (GPSS) – supplying a number of military airfields and with connections to some commercial airports, *i.e.* Stansted and Manchester.

TERMINALS

The United Kingdom has four major land-based terminals through which about two-thirds of the country's crude oil production flows. They are Sullom Voe (Shetlands), Flotta (Orkneys), Kinneil (at the end of the Forties Pipeline System) and Teesside on the east coast. Hamble, another mainland terminal, deals with oil coming from several onshore oilfields in the south of England. These terminals supply more than a third of total crude to UK refineries. The crude oil terminals have some associated storage facilities, but these tend to be limited in size to that needed as an operational buffer between the pipelines and any oil tankers that arrive to take on oil from the terminals.

COMMERCIAL AND RETAIL MARKET

More than 200 companies are involved in the distribution and marketing of oil products in the United Kingdom, ranging from oil companies, supermarket and retail chains to small, independent retailers. The market is split into commercial and retail sectors, and is characterised by low profit margins and a high degree of competition.

The commercial market includes power generators, industrial users, transport (aviation, marine and road), agricultural customers and independent fuel distributors (transport and heating fuels). The retail market covers fuels mainly sold from the country's 8 471 filling stations (as of end of 2010). The number of filling stations has more than halved since 1990. Thousands of stations are owned by independent dealers, while the major suppliers (BP, Chevron, Esso, Murco and Shell) own roughly 1 600 stations. Large supermarkets own around 1 250 stations and supply around 40% of the retail fuel market.

OIL PRICES AND TAXES

The United Kingdom operates an open and competitive market where the wholesale price of petroleum products is set by market dynamics. The government influences retail prices for consumers solely through taxation. Compared with other IEA member countries, unleaded petrol prices in the United Kingdom are close to the median

(Figure 15); retail automotive diesel prices are among the highest (Figure 16), while heating oil is relatively cheap (Figure 17). These differences are largely explained by differences in fuel taxation across countries.

As in most IEA member countries, taxes on transport fuels are a major source of government revenue in the United Kingdom. Petrol and diesel are charged an equal fixed duty (announced on a budget-by-budget basis), currently 57.95 pence per litre. Petrol and diesel are also subject to value-added tax (VAT), at a rate of 20% since March 2011. VAT on diesel is refunded for commercial users. Diesel and petrol excise taxes and VAT have been on equal levels for many years. The government decided in 2011 that the fuel duty would be increased year-on-year by the rate of inflation only, as long as oil prices remain high.

Figure 15. **Unleaded petrol prices and taxes in IEA countries, 4th quarter 2011**

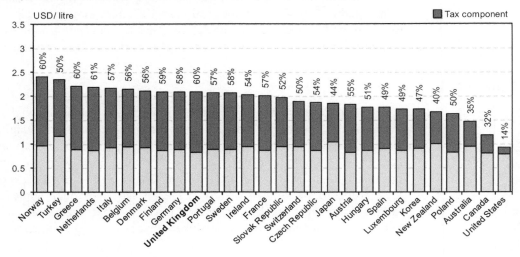

Source: *Energy Prices and Taxes*, IEA/OECD Paris, 2011.

Figure 16. **Automotive diesel prices and taxes in IEA countries, 4th quarter 2011**

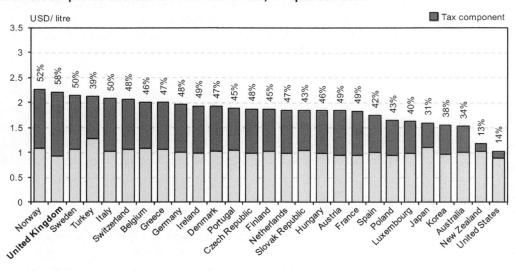

Note: Data not available for Canada.

Source: *Energy Prices and Taxes*, IEA/OECD Paris, 2011.

Figure 17. **Light fuel oil prices and taxes for households in IEA countries, 4th quarter 2011**

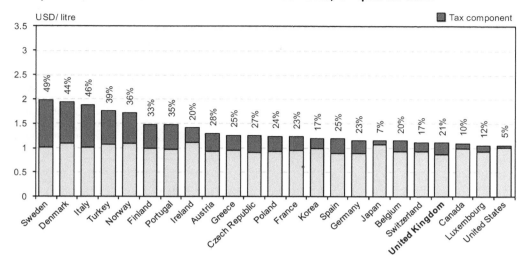

Note: Data are not available for Australia, Hungary, the Netherlands, New Zealand and the Slovak Republic.

Source: *Energy Prices and Taxes,* IEA/OECD Paris, 2011.

Diesel prices at the pump were much higher than unleaded petrol until mid-2009, partly owing to a tighter market for diesel in Europe, partly because diesel costs slightly more to produce. This, and relatively high taxes on diesel, have shielded the United Kingdom from the "dieselisation" that has affected the vehicle fleets of many European countries over the last decade.

SECURITY OF OIL SUPPLY

STOCKHOLDING REGIME

The United Kingdom meets its IEA stockholding obligation by placing compulsory stocking requirements on oil companies operating in the United Kingdom under powers in the Energy Act of 1976 (Table 6). The United Kingdom also has an EU oil-stocking obligation and, in line with other IEA/EU member states, uses the same stocks to meet both obligations.

Companies that supplied petroleum products to the inland UK market (production and net imports) in the previous four-calendar quarters have a stocking obligation. Refining companies must hold stocks equivalent to 67.5 days of their supplies during the previous four quarters, while importing companies must hold stocks equivalent to 58 days. These stocks are commingled with company operating stocks. Other stocks, predominantly those held abroad, also contribute towards the UK total. The United Kingdom has formal bilateral stockholding agreements with Denmark, Ireland, Sweden and the Netherlands. It also has informal agreements with France and Belgium.

The Department of Energy and Climate Change (DECC) is responsible for co-ordinating the response to oil supply emergencies. In addition to the lowering of stockholding obligations on industry, the country would also resort to demand restraint policies.

Table 6. **Legal basis for oil security measures in the United Kingdom**

Legislation	Powers
Energy Act of 1976	**Emergency response organisations** The Energy Act 1976 provides powers, subject to an Order in Council, for the Secretary of State for Energy and Climate Change to regulate or prohibit the production, supply, acquisition or use of fuel where there exists, or is imminent, an actual or threatened emergency in the United Kingdom affecting fuel supplies, or in order for the United Kingdom to meet its international obligations in the event of a reduction or threatened reduction in fuel supplies. These powers are the basis for DECC's authority to function as the UK National Emergency Supply Organisation (NESO). **Stockholding** The Act provides powers for the Secretary of State to direct "any person who…produces, supplies or uses crude liquid petroleum, or petroleum products" to hold stocks of such products based on "quantities…supplied…to the United Kingdom market in past periods". **Implementation of stockdraw and other emergency measures** The powers provided by the Act allow the government to implement stockdraw by companies or take other measures.

Source: *Oil and Gas Security: Emergency Response of IEA Countries – United Kingdom 2010* (update), IEA/OECD Paris, 2010.

The United Kingdom has been consistently compliant with its IEA stockholding obligations. As of September 2011, emergency stocks equalled 442 days of net imports. Before 2006, the United Kingdom was a net exporter and therefore had no stockholding obligation for IEA requirements.

As the country's oil production is decreasing, net imports are set to rise significantly in the coming years and, consequently, its stockholding obligations to the IEA and the EU are expected to rise progressively. Under the EU Directive of 14 September 2009 on crude oil and petroleum product stockholding obligations (Council Directive 2009/119/EC), the United Kingdom is obliged to hold "90 days of average daily net imports or 61 days of average daily inland consumption, whichever of the two quantities is greater". The United Kingdom's 90-day IEA obligation is not expected to overtake the consumption-based EU obligation until around 2020. The switch to calculating the United Kingdom's minimum stockholding requirements on the basis of the IEA/EU 90-day obligation will indicate a growing necessity to hold proportionately more stocks than previously.

STOCK DRAWDOWN

The United Kingdom has the following six-stage process to activate the drawdown of oil stocks. For small domestic incidents, the process can be short-circuited and activated faster.

Stage 1 – Incidence

DECC would alert Cabinet ministers as soon as it was notified of any significant incident that could lead to an oil supply crisis, either within the United Kingdom or worldwide.

DECC would evaluate its intelligence related to the incident in combination with other information, such as the IEA *Preliminary Assessment* for a global disruption, to decide whether a stock release was required. If so, DECC would set up the Joint Response Team (JRT) to evaluate the situation and advise the Director-General for Energy Markets and Infrastructure. Subsequently, the JRT would alert the DECC Secretary of State (SoS) and other government departments. For a UK domestic situation, the JRT would assess the need for and scale of a stockdraw.

Stage 2 – IEA collective action

The JRT would seek the SoS's formal agreement regarding an IEA *Initial Response Plan* within a 24-hour time-frame and would calculate exactly how the United Kingdom would meet its expected contribution to the IEA collective action (essentially through a reduction in days of obligation). The JRT would also alert industry trade associations and co-ordinate a press briefing.

Stage 3 – Activation

Once the IEA *Notice of Activation* has been issued, the JRT would hold an emergency meeting or teleconference with industry stakeholders to inform them of action and the government's role in broad terms before separate bilateral discussions with individual obliged companies.

Stage 4 – Implementation and monitoring

The JRT would contact all compulsory stock obligation (CSO) holders to reduce their obligation levels and set up monitoring arrangements. Companies would be asked to decide upon their individual implementation plans and advise the DECC. Stocks would be expected to be drawn down within an agreed time-frame (usually a month). Monitoring arrangements would be agreed to demonstrate that obligations had been reduced and additional stocks made available to the market. Depending on the incident, the DECC could collect weekly or monthly data. Weekly stock data were collected during the Hurricane Katrina Collective Action and the Libya Collective Action.

During a domestic crisis, the JRT would continuously evaluate the drawdown to consider the need for releasing additional stocks or to terminate the action. For a global disruption, the JRT would follow the IEA's lead.

Stage 5 – Termination of stock drawdown

Following the decision to terminate the drawdown (either following agreement at the IEA Governing Board or a JRT decision for a domestic crisis), the JRT would immediately contact CSO holders and agree a transition period for companies to rebuild stocks to their obligation level. The JRT itself would be disbanded with a "hotwash" to collect issues that arose.

Stage 6 – Review

DECC would review the United Kingdom's drawdown of stocks or its contribution to the IEA collective action so as to identify lessons learned and develop/incorporate improvements in its emergency policies, plans and processes.

OIL DEMAND RESTRAINT

Policy and legal instruments

The National Emergency Plan for Fuel (NEP-F) contains the response tools for any measures the Administration may decide to take in order to quickly reduce oil demand. Indeed, it is designed to help reduce demand for fuel by rationing to ordinary motorists and ensures that fuel is prioritised to critical services. Use of some elements of the NEP-F will require emergency powers to be taken under the Energy Act 1976. The key objectives of the NEP-F are to:

- protect human life and, as far as possible, property, and alleviate suffering;

- support the continuity of everyday activity and the restoration of disrupted services at the earliest opportunity; and

- uphold the rule of law and democratic process.

Should it be necessary to use emergency powers under the Energy Act 1976, the government would prioritise fuel to the emergency services and other essential service providers such as utility companies. The objective is to make the best use of reduced quantities of fuel and to minimise the impact on emergency and other essential services that underpin daily life. If there is sufficient diesel to supply emergency and other essential service providers, then the surplus will be prioritised to truck stops and some motorway filling stations for heavy goods vehicles to help keep supply chains operational. Any remaining fuel would then be allocated by the oil industry to retail filling stations, where it is likely that motorists would be limited to a maximum purchase of fuel per visit to the forecourt.

Measures and procedures

The United Kingdom has a clearly defined demand restraint programme, and a clear legal mandate to implement. The main response tools within the NEP-F are:

- *The maximum purchase scheme* would limit the general public to 15 litres of fuel per visit (though this is variable). This is designed to ensure that all motorists have access to some fuel.

- *Designated filling stations (DFS)* would provide priority access to road transport fuels for defined customers requiring them to deliver critical services. The Department of Energy and Climate Change (DECC) would implement the scheme designating a number of filling stations for the provision of fuel for the emergency services scheme and the utilities fuel scheme for priority use only. Fuel suppliers/distributors will be instructed to give priority deliveries of fuel to these sites.

- *The commercial scheme* prioritises diesel supply to commercial filling stations and truck stops to support the continuation of critical supply chains.

- *The emergency services scheme*, under which fuel would be obtained from designated filling stations and would allow unlimited fuel to blue light emergency vehicles.

- *The utilities fuel scheme*, under which fuel would be obtained from designated filling stations for use by logoed vehicles in the delivery of pre-identified essential services.

- *The bulk distribution scheme* enables oil companies and distributors to prioritise fuel products to supply retail filling stations, truck stops, depots and commercial storage sites.

- *Mutual aid,* under which the DECC has encouraged organisations to develop voluntary mutual aid arrangements to support the delivery of essential services.

Volumetric savings and monitoring

The UK Administration indicates that it is difficult to assess the potential volumetric savings that these policies could make. Experience suggests that when a potential disruption is announced, demand surges can lead to panic buying. Consequently, DECC has developed its response tools to manage the surge in demand and mitigate panic buying to ensure that key services have sufficient fuel to keep the economy running.

DECC has flexible monitoring arrangements with the main industry and trade associations to capture quantitative and qualitative information. There is a generic reporting template that can be modified according to the situation. Reporting is on a daily basis, covering the previous 24 hours, but also including a forward look facility to highlight potential issues.

Daily reporting was successfully used during the Grangemouth and tanker driver disputes in 2008 when it helped monitor regional supply levels at filling stations and the level of stock-outs (stations running out of particular fuels or grades). Local area reporting from regional resilience teams also exists during a crisis to supplement industry reporting.

NATURAL GAS OVERVIEW

Natural gas is the largest energy source in the United Kingdom, accounting for 42% of total primary energy supply (TPES) in 2010. This is one of the highest shares among IEA member countries. With a demand of 85 Mtoe (99 billion cubic metres) in 2010, the United Kingdom is one of the largest gas consumers in Europe. Future demand of gas will heavily depend on developments in the country's power generating capacity.

After being a net exporter of natural gas between 1995 and 2003, the United Kingdom became a net importer in 2004. The country has been enhancing its import infrastructure since then. Imports are relatively diversified between pipeline imports from Norway, the Netherlands and other European countries and liquefied natural gas (LNG) imports from various sources. The United Kingdom also exports gas to Ireland and to continental Europe via the Interconnector (IUK). Since peaking in 2000, natural gas production has been declining, although unconventional gas could increase in importance.

The United Kingdom has been a leader in energy market liberalisation, which started in the early 1990s. All consumers were provided the opportunity to choose their gas supplier as early as 1998. Retail market consolidation has increased over the last decade and six electricity and gas suppliers now dominate the market. Meanwhile, ownership unbundling of the transmission system operator was implemented well ahead of the deadlines set by the European Union gas market directives.

NATURAL GAS SUPPLY AND DEMAND

SUPPLY

Proven natural gas reserves have declined over the last decade from 1.2 trillion cubic metres (tcm) in 2000 to 253 billion cubic metres (bcm) at the end of 2010, according to DECC. Current proven reserves equal only roughly five times the current annual production. In addition to proven reserves, the country also has probable reserves, estimated by DECC at 267 bcm, and possible reserves estimated at 261 bcm. Total resources thus amount to 781 bcm, of which 44% are from condensate fields, 40% from dry gas fields and the rest is associated gas. Cumulative gas production was 2 337 bcm at the end of 2010 (Table 5).

Domestic gas production declined fast from 2000 to 2010, by more than 6% per year. In 2010, total gas production was 59.8 bcm or 51.5 Mtoe, barely half of the level in 2000 (115.4 bcm) (Figure 18). The government forecasts this decline to continue and net gas production to drop to 38.2 bcm by 2016.[4] DECC projects import dependence to increase from around 41% in 2010 to more than 65% by 2025.

UK gas production comes 99.9% from offshore fields, mostly from the North Sea, but also from the Irish Sea. The west of Shetland area is believed to hold significant resources. The Laggan and Tormore fields will be the first gas fields in that area to be developed, with a new gas export pipeline from the Shetland Islands linked to the existing infrastructure to St. Fergus. Initial plateau production is expected to amount to 5 bcm per year.

Figure 18. **Indigenous net gas production and net exports, 1973 to 2010**

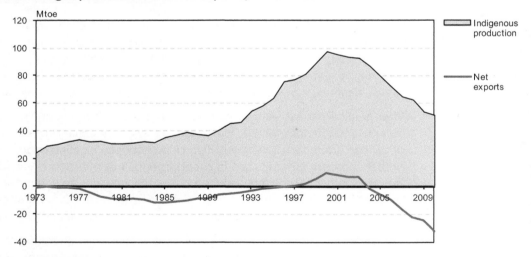

Source: *Natural Gas Information*, IEA/OECD Paris, 2011.

Part of the gas production is dry (non-associated) and depends strongly on gas demand variations, while associated gas production tends to have a "flatter" profile during the year (excluding maintenance periods). However, with the decline of domestic gas

4. http://og.decc.gov.uk/assets/og/data-maps/chapters/production-projections.pdf. Central case. September 2011.

production, dry gas production has been dropping as well and, more importantly, the seasonal production spread is narrowing (Figure 19). Production has collapsed in swing fields that have been used as an alternative to storage, owing to their ability to rapidly ramp up production during winter. A case in point is Morecambe in the Irish Sea, where production dropped from 8.4 bcm in 2000 to 3.7 bcm in 2010.

The United Kingdom could hold some unconventional gas resources, notably coal-bed methane (CBM) and shale gas. The United States Energy Information Administration estimates that recoverable shale gas resources amount to more than 500 bcm. However, unconventional gas production faces many challenges, including local opposition owing to possible environmental impact and water management issues.

Figure 19. **Dry and associated gross natural gas production**

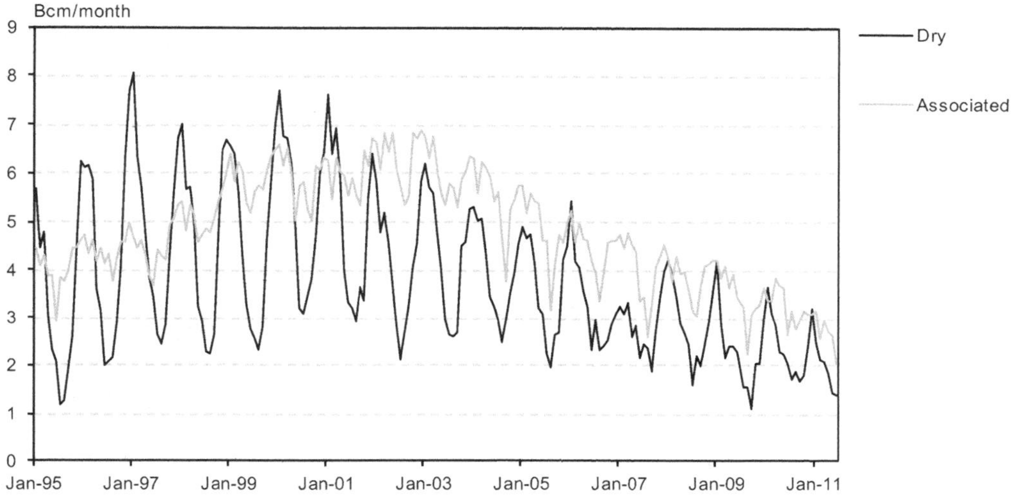

Sources: Department of Energy and Climate Change; *Oil and Gas Information*, IEA/OECD Paris, 2011.

IMPORTS AND EXPORTS

Natural gas imports began in the mid-1960s and the United Kingdom was among the first LNG importers. Imports picked up in the early 1980s with the commissioning of the first pipeline from Norway. From 1977 to 1995, the United Kingdom was a net importer. Then it was a net exporter until 2003. Since 2004, the United Kingdom has been a net importer and imported quantities increased with the development of new pipelines and, since 2005, LNG import infrastructure (Box 3).

In 2010, around 54 bcm of gas were imported, mainly from Norway (48% of the total), Qatar (27%) and the Netherlands (15%). Other suppliers included Algeria, Nigeria and Trinidad and Tobago. Most gas has been imported by pipeline, with the volume ranging from 31 bcm to 36 bcm over the past three years. LNG imports have increased dramatically from 3.5 bcm in 2006 to 18.5 bcm in 2010 and continued on an increasing trend to reach 14.6 bcm in the first half of 2011. This growth reflects both the increase of LNG import capacity and the dramatic expansion in global liquefaction capacity by 100 bcm in 2009 and 2010. Qatar, one of the key suppliers to the United Kingdom, saw its annual export capacity triple to 105 bcm from April 2009 to February 2011.

Box 3. **LNG import infrastructure in the United Kingdom**

Facing the rapid decline of domestic production, the United Kingdom had to increase its import capacity while diversifying supply sources. Besides pipelines, four new LNG import terminals came into operation between July 2005 and 2010. Annual LNG import capacity was 56 bcm by the end of 2011.

The first of these LNG import terminals, the 4.5 bcm Isle of Grain facility, was commissioned in July 2005. It is owned by the National Grid, the transmission system operator. Several companies contracted the terminal's capacity on a long-term basis. BP and Sonatrach have contracted the first phase for 20 years. The Isle of Grain terminal has been expanded twice: in December 2008 (by 9 bcm) and December 2010 (by a further 6.8 bcm). The capacity of the first expansion was contracted, also on a long-term basis, by Sonatrach, GDF-SUEZ and Centrica; and capacity of the second expansion was contracted by E.ON Ruhrgas, Iberdrola and Centrica. The regulations for the Isle of Grain terminal require the primary capacity holders to offer to sell spare import capacity (berthing slots, space and deliverability) to secondary users.

As the United Kingdom gas market faced unprecedented tightness from late 2005 to late 2006, a 4.1 bcm floating offshore regasification terminal was built in Teesside by Excelerate. Construction time for the Teesside GasPort was very short and the terminal was put into operation in February 2007.

The South Hook LNG import terminal at Milford Haven is by far the largest in the United Kingdom with two phases of 10.5 bcm each, commissioned in March 2009 and April 2010. Promoted by Qatar Petroleum (67.5%), ExxonMobil (24.15%) and Total (8.35%), this terminal receives large volumes of Qatari LNG. The terminal's operators were granted a 20-year exemption from third-party access (TPA). Nevertheless, three third parties – ConocoPhillips, EGL and Trafigura – were granted access to spare import capacity in 2011.

The 6 bcm Dragon terminal located near South Hook was commissioned in 2009. The terminal is owned by BG and Petronas (50% each) and has a 20-year TPA exemption.

Plans for additional LNG import terminals exist. Among the proposed projects are further expansions of the Isle of Grain and Dragon facilities, as well as new LNG terminals in Teesside or Anglesey. With a projected 60% utilisation of its LNG import capacity in 2011, the United Kingdom has some reserve capacity.

The United Kingdom also exports a part of its production, 15.3 bcm in 2010, supplying gas to continental Europe (10.2 bcm) and Ireland (5.1 bcm). Exports to continental Europe have increased over the past three years in line with UK LNG imports. The United Kingdom is effectively turning into a gateway for LNG to the continental market.

DEMAND

Total natural gas demand in the United Kingdom reached 99 bcm (85 Mtoe) in 2010. This is slightly below the record of 102 bcm in 2000, but a clear increase from 91 bcm in 2009. The largest consuming sectors are power generation and households, each accounting for slightly more than a third of the total (Figure 20). The rest was consumed in industry (12%), commercial and public services (6%) and the energy sector (6%).

Because of the high share of gas use for heating, total gas demand varies according to temperature. As 2010 was a relatively cold year (1.1 degrees Celsius cooler than 2009), residential gas demand was 17% higher than the previous year. Preliminary data for 2011 show a 15% drop in total demand, owing to a return to average weather conditions, combined with higher gas prices (absolutely and relative to coal for power generation), improvements in energy efficiency and deteriorating economic conditions.

Gas demand for power generation is particularly sensitive to the relative prices of gas and coal. For example, when gas prices peaked in the winter of 2005/06, power generators switched from gas to coal. In contrast, gas use for power generation was particularly high from late 2009 to April 2010, as gas prices had significantly dropped to around USD 4 to 5 per million British thermal units (MBtu).

The government expects total gas demand to decrease over the coming ten years. This will depend largely on future power demand (for which GDP growth is a key driver), continuing strong growth of renewable energy supply and the relative competitiveness of natural gas against coal at the margin.

Figure 20. **Natural gas demand by sector, 1973 to 2020***

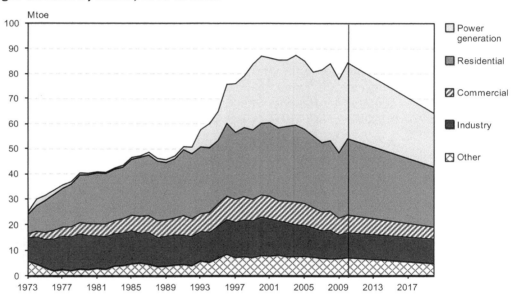

* Total primary energy supply by consuming sector. *Other* includes other transformation and energy sector consumption. *Industry* includes non-energy use. *Commercial* includes commercial, public services, agriculture/ forestry, fishing and other final consumption.

Sources: *Energy Balances of OECD Countries*, IEA/OECD Paris, 2011; country submission.

Natural gas demand in the United Kingdom peaks in winter (Table 7). According to National Grid, average gas demand ranges from 250 to 300 million cubic metres per day (mcm/d), while on an average winter day gas demand is 350 to 400 mcm and on a very cold winter day it could approach 500 mcm.

Peak exit volumes on a daily and monthly basis will depend on such factors as time of year, temperature anomalies, whether gas is the marginal source for power generation, storage injection demand, and export demand from the continent via the interconnector pipeline to Belgium. On an average winter day, peak demand is typically met with a combination of production from the United Kingdom continental shelf, pipeline imports from Norway, the Netherlands and Belgium, LNG imports and withdrawals from storage.

Table 7. **Seasonal natural gas demand, 2005 to 2010**

Demand (billion cubic metres)	2005	2006	2007	2008	2009	2010
Summer*	39.1	35.4	36.6	38.2	33.9	35.7
Winter*	60.7	57.9	60.7	57.5	61.2	62.6
Additional winter demand (%)	55	64	66	51	80	75

* Winter is October to March and summer is April to September.

Source: DECC: *Energy Trends*, table 4.1.

NATURAL GAS INFRASTRUCTURE

TRANSMISSION AND DISTRIBUTION

Natural gas is supplied through a relatively dense pipeline network of around 285 000 kilometres (km) serving almost 23 million users. The high-pressure transmission pipelines transport gas from import points (pipeline or LNG terminals) to major centres of population as well as to some large users, such as gas-fired power plants. These pipelines are called the national transmission system (NTS), which is owned and operated by National Grid Gas (NGG). The transmission system currently consists of 7 600 km of high pressure pipelines. Natural gas infrastructure is shown in Figure 14.

From the NTS, gas is delivered to small users through the distribution network. These users include domestic and business customers, but also the 16 independent gas transporters (IGTs). There are eight gas distribution networks (GDNs) in Great Britain (Northern Ireland is part of the Irish gas market). These networks are operated by five GDN operators (National Grid Gas, Scotland Gas Networks, Northern Gas Networks, Wales & West Utilities and Southern Gas Networks). National Grid Gas owns and operates the distribution network in the North West of England, the West Midlands, East England and North London.

CROSS-BORDER CONNECTIONS

In order to compensate for the decline in production, the United Kingdom has expanded gas import infrastructure in recent years. Three pipelines link the United Kingdom to the Norwegian North Sea fields. The Vesterled pipeline (13 bcm) from the Heimdal field to St. Fergus was the first and started in 1978. The Langeled pipeline (25 bcm) linking the Norwegian Orman Lange field to Easington started operating in 2006, and the Tampen Link (9 bcm) between the Statfjord field and the FLAGS pipeline started in late 2007.

Two pipelines link the United Kingdom to continental Europe – the Interconnector UK, a two-way pipeline that can import up to 25.5 bcm to the United Kingdom and export up to 20 bcm to Belgium, was commissioned in October 1998.[5] The pipeline is generally

---

5. The pipeline capacity was gradually increased from 8.5 bcm in 1998 to 16.5 bcm in November 2005 to 23.5 bcm in October 2006 to reach 25.5 bcm in October 2007.

used for imports in winter and exports in summer. The second import pipeline (one-way) is the Balgzand to Bacton (BBL) pipeline (15 bcm) from the Netherlands that started in December 2006.

STORAGE

The United Kingdom's working storage capacity is currently at 4.4 bcm. The United Kingdom has long relied on domestic production for flexibility, but as this production declines and import dependence increases, storage is becoming more important as a means to provide flexibility. Current underground gas storage facilities are listed in Table 8.

The United Kingdom has three types of gas storage: long-range storage, medium-range storage (typically salt caverns, such as Aldbrough and depleted fields, such as Hatfield Moor) and short-range storage (peak LNG plants). Long-range storage is typically used for seasonal variations. Rough, the only such facility in the United Kingdom currently, represents three-quarters of the country's storage capacity. It is owned and operated by former incumbent Centrica Storage. Medium-range storage facilities are better suited to meet daily variations; they have been developed by UK gas and power players. The peak-shaving units have low working capacity, but very high deliverability and can meet demand peaks during exceptionally cold days.

There are several projects to develop new storage facilities. The planning process, with the involvement of local authorities, has been delaying some projects because of local opposition. The Planning Act of 2008 for nationally significant infrastructure projects and the Energy Act of 2008 aim to improve the planning and consent process. However, the declining spread between summer and winter prices has become more of a consideration for investors. Around 1 bcm of storage projects are currently under construction, to start by 2014.

Table 8. **Underground gas storage facilities, 2011**

Facility	Working capacity (bcm)	Withdrawal rate (mcm per day)	Company
Existing			
Rough	3.3	45	Centrica Storage
Aldbrough	0.2	12	SSE/Statoil
Hatfield Moor	0.1	2	Scottish Power
Holehouse Farm	0.06	7	Energy Merchants Gas Storage (EDF)
Hornsea	0.3	17	SSE Hornsea
Humbly Grove	0.3	7	Star Energy
LNG storage	0.08	13	National Grid LNGS
Under construction			
Aldbrough Ph 2	0.2	25	SSE/Statoil
Hill Top Farm	0.1	15	EDF Trading
Holford	0.2	22	E.ON
Stublach	0.4	32	GDF Storage

Source: *Natural Gas Information*, IEA/OECD Paris, 2011; *Gas Ten Year Statement*, National Grid, 2011.

NATURAL GAS MARKET STRUCTURE AND REGULATION

MARKET STRUCTURE

The United Kingdom obtains natural gas supplies from various sources, including domestic production and imports via pipelines and in the form of LNG. Gas production is relatively well diversified with five companies having a market share above 5%. Market share in pipeline imports is rather difficult to assess owing to secondary trading of capacity. There are 16 shippers who hold primary capacity on the Interconnector UK, seven main shippers on the Langeled pipeline and another seven on the BBL. Six shippers (BP, Centrica, GDF Suez, E.ON Ruhrgas, Iberdrola and Sonatrach) import gas at the Isle of Grain. South Hook and Dragon are mostly used by their owners.

Since market liberalisation in the 1990s, both the retail electricity and gas markets have become more concentrated. Through mergers and acquisitions, the fifteen former incumbent electricity and gas suppliers have been reduced to six main electricity and gas suppliers. In the retail gas market, the big six suppliers (Centrica, E.ON, EDF, ScottishPower, SSE and RWE) have 99.9% of the residential market. Data from late 2009 show that British Gas (owned by Centrica) alone had 48% of the customers, followed by SSE with 16%, and E.ON UK 14%. RWE nPower 12%, Scottish Power (owned by Iberdrola) 9% and EDF Energy 8%. Five small suppliers (First Utility, Good Energy, Utilita, Spark Energy and OVO Energy) hold the remaining 0.1%.

The non-domestic gas market (daily metered, non-daily metered, small businesses) has eight independent suppliers (Corona Energy, ENI, Gazprom, GDF Suez, Shell, Statoil, Total and Wingas) in addition to the big six suppliers. The daily-metered segment is by far the most fragmented, with the top three suppliers (ENI, GDF Suez and Shell) supplying 47% of the total. The non-daily metered segment is much more concentrated as the top three suppliers (Centrica, E.ON Energy and Corona Energy) hold a combined 72% of the market. The small business segment is also rather concentrated, with Centrica, E.ON and SSE holding 79% of the market, with 38% for Centrica alone.

REGULATION

Several laws and regulations are designed to ensure that the UK market provides safe and secure gas supplies for consumers. The main legislation measures are:

- the Gas Act of 1986 is the centrepiece of onshore gas market regulation. It includes the licensing regime for gas transporters, shippers and suppliers, as well as the framework for the exemption regime;

- the Petroleum Act of 1998 provides a licensing regime for onshore and offshore gas production development; it also provides a consent regime for offshore pipelines;

- the Planning Act of 2008 was introduced to create a more efficient planning system for nationally significant infrastructure, including gas supply infrastructure, which is located mostly in England;

- the Energy Act of 2008 establishes a clear regulatory framework for offshore gas storage developments and gas unloading platforms.

Gas market legislation also complies with European Union law. The requirements of the third Gas Market Directive (2009/73/EC) were transposed into national law in September 2011.

Two bodies regulate the gas market: the Office of Gas and Electricity Markets (Ofgem) for Great Britain and the Northern Ireland Authority for Utility Regulation for Northern Ireland. Ofgem is an independent regulator with responsibilities for regulation of transmission and distribution, as well as overseeing competition in the gas and electricity markets. Ofgem derives its powers and duties from several acts, including the Gas Act 1986, Utilities Act 2000, the Energy Acts of 2004, 2008 and 2010, and those from EU law. Notably, Ofgem conducts retail market reviews. The 2011 edition found that additional action was required to help consumers identify the supplier offering the cheapest tariff at a given time. Ofgem has powers under the Competition Act to investigate potential anti-competitive activity in the natural gas and electricity sectors. It is a National Competition Authority under the EU modernisation regulation.

Ofgem regulates the level of charges that National Grid Gas can levy through the Transmission Price Control Review (TPCR). The most recent TPCR sets out proposals to apply typically for five years for each of the transmission licensees in their role as transmission owners (TOs). In 2009, a one-year roll-over of the last TPCR (done in 2007) was announced until 2013.

Ofgem also regulates gas distribution tariffs. The maximum revenue a network may recover from its customers for a specific time period is based on a benchmark, which in turn is based on an analysis of the gas distribution networks' actual costs. The current gas distribution price control period is in effect until March 2013.

SECURITY OF NATURAL GAS SUPPLY

Government policy on security of gas supply is based on the following five pillars:

- maximising economic production from indigenous resources;

- reducing demand for energy by promoting energy efficiency measures;

- utilising well-functioning commodity and capital markets to deliver a high-quality service to consumers and to provide necessary levels of investment across the system;

- complementing and strengthening the operation of the market through regulation; and

- promoting strong and diverse markets, both within the EU and internationally.

In normal conditions, the United Kingdom relies on the gas market to maintain security of supply. Suppliers and shippers are responsible for contracting gas volumes and network capacity to meet consumer demand, while National Grid, the transmission system operator (TSO), is responsible for both ensuring the availability of network capacity to meet anticipated transportation requirements and balancing the market (for both gas and electricity). If the shippers and suppliers fail to balance their positions, they will be subject to the "system buy" and "system sell" imbalance prices, *i.e.* marginal prices in the system. The government generally relies on the market to balance supply and demand, but the country also has specific measures available to respond to gas supply emergencies. These measures include interruptible gas supply contracts, switching from gas to coal for power generation, and storage. The country also has a specific response plan, the National Emergency Plan for Gas & Electricity (NEP-G&E). DECC, Ofgem and NGG work together to closely monitor gas security of supply.

Fuel switching in power generation is the most common response to reductions in gas supply. A shortage of natural gas can be expected to lead to higher wholesale gas prices wherein gas ceases to be the economical fuel choice. Coal-fired power generation is ramped up while gas-fired generation falls. This flexibility in the gas market, however, will be reduced over the next decade, as some 8 gigawatts of coal-fired capacity will have to be closed by 2023 under EU air quality legislation.

Gas-fired power generation can also be replaced through fuel switching at about fifteen combined-cycle gas turbines (CCGTs). The distillate backup capacity of these dual-fired CCGTs is estimated at around 24 mcm per day, but only 114 mcm per month and 500 bcm per year, as restocking limits monthly and annual volumes, according to Pöyry Consulting.[6]

Interruptible gas supply contracts in the industrial and commercial sectors provided an estimated maximum daily interruptible gas capacity of about 36 mcm in 2010. Changes to the rights of these gas customers to discounted transportation charges in October 2011, however, are expected to reduce interest in interruptible contracts and, according to Pöyry Consulting, reduce the available volumes to 10 mcm per day in 2012/13.

The United Kingdom has enhanced and effectively diversified its import infrastructure and currently has 156 bcm per year import capacity, and remains a large producer. Storage capacity has increased over the last decade by around 25% and around 1 bcm of new storage capacity is under construction and expected to be completed by 2014.

Several new initiatives are under way to enable greater demand-side response from the residential sector, such as the introduction of smart meters, smart grids and financial incentives for shorter settlement periods for consumers. However, these may only deliver significant demand-side response capacity in the medium term.

The NEP-G&E sets out the arrangements between the gas and electricity industries, and DECC for the safe and effective management of gas and electricity supply emergencies in Great Britain. (Gas and electricity supply emergencies in Northern Ireland are covered by separate arrangements.) The NEP-G&E could involve the use of Emergency Powers under the Energy Act of 1976, which would only be activated in significant emergencies. The plan applies to:

▪ electricity supply network from generator to consumers' meter or electricity supply terminal; and

▪ downstream gas supply network from reception terminal or storage site to customer isolation valve.

For gas emergencies, the Network Emergency Co-ordinator would direct the gas distribution networks to reduce demand. This is done under industry arrangements independent of the NEP-G&E. Large industrial gas users would be directed either to cease all use or, for protected sites under the Gas Priority User Arrangements, to reduce their gas demand significantly, with the aim of maintaining safe minimum pressures within the gas network. The last customers to be affected would be residences. A volume of gas must be maintained in storage to protect certain vulnerable customers, such as households and hospitals, against a "1 in 50" winter.

---

6. *GB Gas Security of Supply and Options for Improvement. A report to the Department of Energy and Climate Change,* March 2010.

Looking ahead, past experience and DECC's risk assessments show that the gas system generally is very resilient and should remain so. In an April 2010 policy statement on security of gas supply, DECC projects that annual demand can be met up to 2020 and beyond by existing import capacity and projected supply from indigenous resources, and that 2020 peak demand can also be met by existing capacity or that under construction. After 2020, planned infrastructure would provide sufficient capacity to supply the highest peak demand scenarios, even if only a minority of the planned projects are completed.

NATURAL GAS PRICES

WHOLESALE

The wholesale price of gas in Great Britain is the National Balancing Point (NBP) price. Established in 1998, the NBP is the largest and most liquid natural gas spot market in Europe and provides a reference as an alternative to oil indexation. Although the NBP spot market does not have the same liquidity as the Henry Hub in the United States, the ratio between traded and physical deliveries is more than 10 and stood at 14 for early 2011.

The wholesale gas price has varied considerably over the past ten years (Figure 21). As the United Kingdom moved from a net exporter to a net importer in 2004, NBP prices increased from USD 3 to 4 per MBtu to USD 7 per MBtu. The relationship between the NBP and continental (oil-linked) gas prices then changed, so that the NBP became on average higher than continental prices, although they were still lower during summer times. In particular, NBP prices were showing a significant seasonality at that time, and spot prices peaked at high levels during winter 2005/06 (USD 14 to 15 per MBtu), reflecting shortages on the UK market.

Figure 21. **Natural gas wholesale and retail prices, 1997 to 2010**

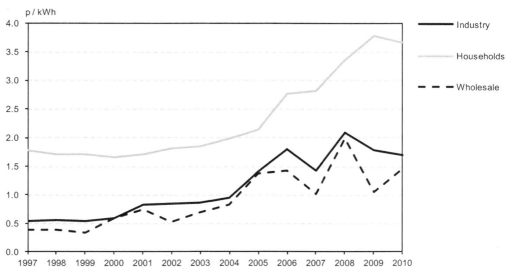

Sources: DECC, IEA.

After a sharp increase in 2008, similar to European and US gas prices, NBP prices collapsed in late 2009, because of the economic crisis, which reduced gas demand at the same time as significant supply was arriving to the market – shale gas in the United States and new LNG. During one year to April 2010, NBP and Henry Hub prices converged at relatively low levels, around USD 4 to 5 per MBtu. Since then, NBP prices rose to almost converge with continental European prices at around USD 9 to 10 per MBtu reflecting tightness on global natural gas markets and the fact that the United Kingdom is now acting as a bridge for more supplies to the wider continental markets. However, NBP prices remain at a discount compared with oil-linked gas prices.

RETAIL

The NBP price is the most important component of end-user price. End-user prices are not controlled by the regulator, but set by the suppliers. Ofgem regulates the transmission and distribution components.

As NBP prices have increased over the past decade, so have end-user gas prices (Figure 21). Industrial gas prices have closely followed NBP price developments and in 2009 were 2.9 times higher than 2000 levels (1.74 pence per kilowatt-hour versus 0.61 p/kWh). Residential gas prices have increased from 1.58 p/kWh in 2000 to 4.2 p/kWh in 2009. Following the increase in wholesale gas prices in late 2010, the six largest suppliers raised retail prices. The effect was that consumer gas bills, which had been declining since February 2009, started to rise in late 2010 and increased quite sharply from mid-2011.[7] Many households are "dual fuel" consumers, which means that they buy their electricity and gas from the same supplier.

One notable pattern is that the seasonal pattern is less pronounced than past observations. It may happen that gas prices are higher in the summer than in the winter. Overall, the winter-summer spread has been narrowing, which is weakening the signal to invest in new storage options.

By international comparison, retail natural gas prices for both household and industrial customers are low (Figures 22 and 23). In recent years, UK residential and industrial users have also benefited from having one of the lowest tax rates on gas consumption among the IEA member countries.

7. Ofgem, *Electricity and Gas Supply Market Report*, October 2011.

Figure 22. **Natural gas prices in IEA countries, 2010**

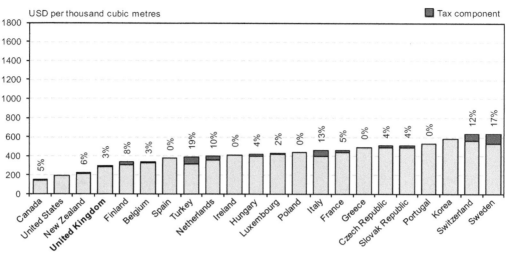

Note: Tax information is not available for Korea and the United States. Data are not available for Australia, Austria, Denmark, Germany, Japan and Norway.

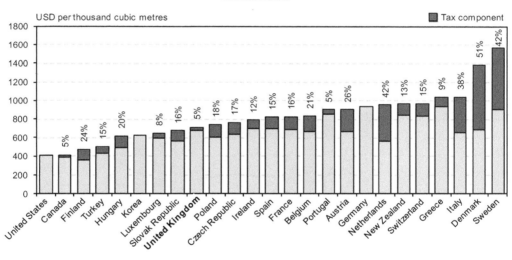

Note: Tax information is not available for Germany, Korea and the United States. Data are not available for Australia, Japan and Norway.

Source: Energy Prices and Taxes, IEA/OECD Paris, 2011.

Figure 23. **Retail natural gas prices in the United Kingdom and in selected IEA countries, 1990 to 2010**

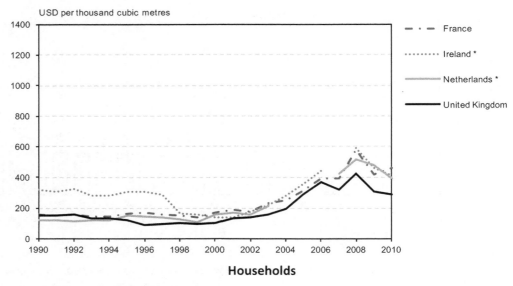

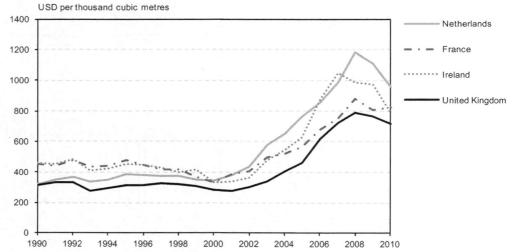

* Data partially not available.

Source: *Energy Prices and Taxes*, IEA/OECD Paris, 2011.

CRITIQUE

OIL AND NATURAL GAS PRODUCTION

Today fossil fuels dominate the United Kingdom's energy sector and will remain crucial to the country's near- and mid-term energy future. Oil and natural gas reserves are in decline as a result of exploration and production on a maturing continental shelf. Import dependence on these fuels is increasing. Although production is forecast to decline sharply in coming decades, the remaining petroleum resources are sufficient to provide major benefits to the UK economy and to security of supply for many years.

Government policy in the upstream hydrocarbons sector aims to maximise the economic recovery from the country's oil and gas reserves, taking full account of environmental, social and economic objectives. To address the challenges posed by a maturing petroleum province, regulations have been adjusted to exploit fallow, marginal and previously unproven resources, while ensuring a fair return for the taxpayer. The government is to be commended for its policy initiatives in this area over the last decade.

Several challenges remain in the upstream sector, both for the petroleum industry and for the government. These relate to bringing additional resources into production, new operators with limited operational experience and global cost increases in upstream activities. On a positive note, increased recovery from existing fields offers significant revenue potential. However, decommissioning costs may reduce the liquidity of the asset transfer market, and should continue to be a focus area for the government.

Recent changes in the upstream tax regime have raised some concerns, owing to increased divergence between oil and gas prices. This is an area where continued monitoring of gas developments and production may be needed.

Upstream petroleum activities are characterised by long lead times. Predictability through stable fiscal regimes is believed to influence the competitiveness of different petroleum provinces. Continued investments will be vital to utilise remaining petroleum resources on the UK continental shelf. The government should therefore seek stability in the upstream regime to promote continued investments.

DOWNSTREAM OIL

The oil sector will continue to have a vital role in the UK economy by providing the required transport fuels and associated infrastructure to produce, import and distribute fuels. The sector will help to decarbonise the economy, notably the transport sector, *e.g.* by ensuring the successful blending of biofuels and the introduction of new fuel grades on the market. However, for several years now, there has been a lack of growth in demand and generally poor margins in the industry that have resulted in little discretionary investment. The key investment driver has been compliance with regulatory requirements.

In the refining sector, some formerly integrated international oil companies (IOCs) have restructured their asset portfolios; BP and Shell have effectively withdrawn from refining. IOCs in the United Kingdom and elsewhere in the EU have reduced their exposure to refining largely because of depressed refining markets, an overall excess of international refining capacity, and more attractive international investment opportunities. At the same time, new companies have entered the refining business in the United Kingdom, with differing business models and ownership structures. That new investors wish to invest in the United Kingdom can be seen as an encouraging sign of the underlying attractiveness of the UK refining sector.

On the basis of its current level of refining capacity, the United Kingdom may remain a net exporter of refined products for the foreseeable future. However, a mismatch between the country's refinery product output and its petroleum product demand means that the country is currently a net importer of aviation fuel and middle distillates/diesel, while it is a net exporter of fuel oil and gasoline. In the future, aviation fuel and diesel are likely to increase their share in the country's oil mix. This is in part because of several pieces of EU legislation and of the International Maritime

Organization's (MARPOL VI) proposals for marine bunker fuels at significantly reduced sulphur levels, which have increased the need for middle distillates production since the use of heavy fuel oil as bunker fuel would be discontinued. The UK petroleum industry needs to decide how much to rely on imports and how much to invest in changing its refining upgrading capacity to respond to this trend.

In the retail fuels sector, the number of filling stations has more than halved since 1990. Many of the supermarkets that engage in fuel retailing have higher than average throughput (more than 3.5 million litres per year) to the point that the supermarkets supply about 40% of the retail fuel market. The majority of the retail sites are supplied from primary distribution terminals operated by the six major oil companies, although independent traders and fuel suppliers are of increasing importance and have secured significant supply to the supermarket chains with imported product.

In light of these developments, market concentration may still increase further, leaving certain regions with still fewer fuel suppliers. Longer delivery distances, fewer suppliers, a smaller number of key terminals and/or alternative supply points increase the risks of potential supply disruptions. Small depots and terminals may not attract the required investment and could close. This would put more pressure on the hub locations and imply longer delivery distances and an extended supply chain that may be more vulnerable to disruption. On the other hand, smaller fuel supply companies are entering the market and increasing their market presence, such as Greenergy. Also, a vertically integrated IOC may withdraw from refining but retain its fuel marketing interests, for example Shell or BP, establishing product supply either from an existing indigenous refiner, *e.g.* the new refinery owner, or supplying imported products.

The introduction of new biofuel grades, such as B10/E10, may require additional investment in the provision for a fourth fuel grade on retail service station forecourts to preserve the availability of E5 gasoline for older vehicles unable to use E10. It may also require additional depot storage capacity because of the lower energy content in biofuels.

The United Kingdom does not have a public stockholding agency and does not hold public stocks. The country's minimum stockholding requirements are met by placing obligations on industry. With domestic North Sea oil and gas production set to decline by around 50% from 2010 to 2020, and thus import dependence set to increase, this could create requirements for additional storage capacity in the medium term. In order to assess future infrastructure requirements and plan for any future crises, a clear understanding of the country's current storage capacity is necessary.

The financial costs of setting up a public stock agency are high, particularly in light of the country's current economic situation. Nevertheless, an industry-based agency could be set up at minimal cost, with the costs of stockholding being factored into the oil supply chain and ultimately borne by the end-consumers.

In case of purely domestic disruptions, the United Kingdom has a well-developed and detailed programme for oil supply demand restraint.

DOWNSTREAM NATURAL GAS

The United Kingdom has been a prime mover in terms of natural gas market liberalisation. The national gas company was privatised in 1986 and unbundled in 1995. The full opening of the gas market was completed in 1996. The government has since consistently adhered to free market principles. This has resulted in a very liquid and well-functioning wholesale gas market, such that it is now a model for the rest of Europe. The marketplace for gas, the National Balancing Point (NBP), has a churn rate of well over 10. Over the past three years, the resulting natural gas prices have been on average lower than oil-linked gas prices.

The United Kingdom has also managed to attract large investments in new import infrastructure to counterbalance rapidly declining domestic gas production. Since the country became a net importer in 2004, two new pipelines have been built, one was expanded and four LNG terminals commissioned. At around 156 bcm, total import capacity is considerably higher than annual demand. Seen from this angle, government policy to rely primarily on the market to ensure security of supply has been successful.

However, market-based actions of individual suppliers to respond to security of supply challenges may not be sufficient from a wide gas system perspective. For instance, market players may individually accept low chance-short duration portfolio problems that they intend to solve via the market, but collectively this behaviour may result in supply problems for the country. Furthermore, building new seasonal or peak storage capacity has been slow, while the supply flexibility from domestic gas production is diminishing fast. This is notable because of the declining winter-summer price spread and limited short-term price volatility. The government, including the regulator Ofgem, is considering to take action on these issues by removing the cap on the cash-out price in case of insufficient supply into the grid by a shipper. The recent clarification on taxation of cushion gas and the possible obligations for storage investment should further improve the security of gas supply.

Security of supply does not necessarily imply a need for energy independence, while reliance on imports may be acceptable. In a large number of supplying countries, government involvement in the natural gas market is substantial. Therefore, import reliance goes hand in hand with energy dialogue with the authorities in supplying countries.

As with the wholesale market, the retail market is functioning quite well, but remains rather concentrated. The fact that customers may switch supplier is helping households to keep the suppliers in check, but improvements in several areas would be welcome. These include: the transparency of contracts and pricing schemes; marketing standards; the position of new entrants in a market dominated by vertically and horizontally (with electricity) integrated companies; and the relation between wholesale and retail pricing.

Natural gas is an important source of security of electricity supply. In light of the diminishing role for coal-fired power and the growing need for wind power backup capacity, the role of gas-fired power is set to increase. It will be important that the gas market delivers the necessary infrastructure (including storage capacity) and suppliers to enable flexible gas-fired generation to meet peak electricity demand. The government should develop policies that encourage efficient and timely industry responses to address this issue.

RECOMMENDATIONS

The government of the United Kingdom should:

Oil and natural gas production

☐ *Continue to encourage the development of domestic reserves by implementing additional favourable fiscal and regulatory incentives, as appropriate, to promote continued upstream investments.*

☐ *Continue to monitor gas recovery and consider taking action to counter adverse effects, owing to relatively low natural gas prices in comparison with oil prices.*

Downstream oil

☐ *Improve security of supply by monitoring closely market developments, including those of biofuels, and sustaining constructive dialogue with industry players.*

☐ *Conduct a detailed study of the country's oil storage capacity that would establish details of existing storage capacity, together with a breakdown of the geographical spread of storage within the country; this study would also provide guidance on future storage requirements, taking into account the outlook for future stock obligations.*

☐ *Consider alternative mechanisms to meet international stockholding obligations, including the creation of a compulsory stockholding obligations agency with a clear supply resilience remit, as recommended in the 2010 IEA Emergency Response Review.*

☐ *Conduct studies with a view to quantifying the estimated volumetric impact of specific oil demand restraint measures.*

Downstream natural gas

☐ *Continue to monitor the security of gas supply and emergency response situation: determine the desired level of security of supply; assess the potential of the market to deliver; remove any impediments to investment in new gas supplies and storage; and fine-tune policies to fill possible gaps between the desired and the market-delivered level of security of supply.*

☐ *Continue regular dialogue with the United Kingdom's principal gas suppliers and with potential sources of future supply.*

☐ *Take steps to improve the functioning of the retail market, such as increasing transparency of contracts and pricing schemes, and contract innovation by encouraging new entrants, while adhering to the free market principles.*

6. COAL

Key data (2010)

Production: 17.8 million tonnes of hard coal (11 Mtoe)

Net imports: 25.8 million tonnes of hard coal: 37% from Russia, 24% Colombia, 17% United States and 12% Australia

Contribution to energy supply: 15% of TPES and 29% of electricity generation

Consumption: Power and heat generation 82%, other transformation 10%, industry 5%, households 2%

SUPPLY, DEMAND, TRADE AND OUTLOOK

SUPPLY

In 2010, total coal supply amounted to 51 million tonnes (31 Mtoe), up 3.4% from the historical low in 2009. Since 1990, total coal supply has decreased by more than half (Figure 24). The government projects a further 30% decrease by 2020. Coal's decline is compensated by a large increase in the supply of natural gas, which overtook coal in 1993 to become the second-largest fuel in the United Kingdom. In 2010, coal provided 15% of TPES, significantly lower than the IEA average of 20.6%.

Resources and reserves

According to Euracoal estimates, hard coal reserves in the United Kingdom amount to 600 Mt and coal resources three billion tonnes. The country's coal resources are the second-largest in Europe after Poland, and dwarf the country's conventional oil and gas resources.

Hard coal deposits are found in twelve areas, with working mines in South Wales, Warwickshire, the English North Midlands, Yorkshire, North East England, and the Central Belt of Scotland (Figure 26). At current production rates, the United Kingdom's coal reserves would last more than 33 years.

Production

In 2010, domestic coal production was 17.8 Mt (11 Mtoe), one-fifth of the 1990 level, and 35% of total coal supply, while imports and stock changes covered the rest. The use of stocks built up in 2009 provided a significant 7.2 Mt, or 14% of total supply in 2010.

There is no brown coal production. Indigenous hard coal production has declined significantly over the past four decades, from around 200 Mt in 1950 to an all-time low of around 18 Mt in 2008. Today, around 41% of this production is from underground mines, compared with around 50% in 2005. Between 2005 and 2010, a loss of output from four deep mines which closed or were put into "care and maintenance" status has been largely replaced by improved output from remaining deep mines and by some recovery in surface mine output in England.

Domestic hard coal production has halved over the last decade. This mostly reflects the often poor economics of mining hard coal in the United Kingdom in relation to internationally traded coal, as domestic hard coal demand only dropped by 12% over the period.

However, the United Kingdom is the world's fifteenth-largest and Europe's second-largest hard coal producer. It accounts for 14% of European Union hard coal production (the other EU hard coal producers are Poland, the Czech Republic, Germany, Spain and Romania). As the United Kingdom's indigenous coal has a relatively high sulphur content of 0.6% to 2.5%, most coal-fired power plants have been fitted with flue-gas desulphurisation equipment to meet obligatory emission limits.

According to the UK Coal Authority, 32 surface mines and 14 underground mines are currently in operation or under development. The major coal producer is UK Coal plc, which accounts for around 50% of total coal output. UK Coal operates three large deep mines located in central and northern England and these have substantial reserves. It also operates six surface mines. Other major surface mine operators in England include ATH Resources, HJ Banks & Co Ltd, Celtic Energy, Kier Mining and Miller-Argent.

Prospects for investment in new coal production are low, particularly for underground mines where up-front investments are significant. However, according to the Department of Energy and Climate Change (DECC), UK coal producers can maintain their current output levels of 17 Mt to 18 Mt per year until at least 2020.

Figure 24. **Coal demand by sector, 1973 to 2020***

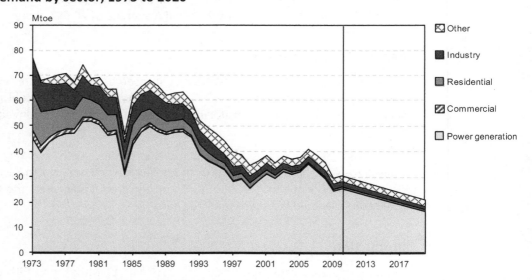

* Total primary energy supply by consuming sector. *Other* includes other transformation and energy sector consumption. *Industry* includes non-energy use. *Commercial* includes residential, commercial, public services, agriculture/forestry, fishing and other final consumption.

Sources: *Energy Balances of OECD Countries,* IEA/OECD Paris, 2011; country submission.

Productivity

According to the UK Coal Authority, the mining sector employed 6 000 workers in 2009, of which around 3 800 worked in England, 1 300 in Scotland and 900 in Wales. Around 3 500 of the total worked in underground mines.

The decline in underground mining has contributed to a steady increase in overall productivity (Figure 25). Also, productivity in the remaining underground mines has increased more than fourfold since the mid-1980s. Today, coal mines in the United Kingdom produce on average almost 3 000 tonnes per man-year. This is higher than in other European countries, such as Poland with an average of 645 tonnes per man-year, but much less than in Australia and the United States where 8 000 to 10 000 tonnes per man-year are normal. Coal-mining productivity is generally much lower in Europe than in the major coal-exporting countries, such as Australia, Colombia, Indonesia and South Africa. This is primarily because Europe has fewer opencast mines and more difficult geological conditions in underground mines.

Figure 25. **Coal mine productivity and number of mines, 1950 to 2010**

Note: Productivity levels reflect end-of-year status of employment, whereas employment might vary over the whole year.

Sources: UK Coal Authority, 2011; IEA statistics.

DEMAND

Power generation is by far the largest coal-consuming sector in the United Kingdom, using 42 Mt (25 Mtoe) of coal, or 82% of total supply in 2010, and producing 109 terawatt-hours (TWh) or 28.8% of total electricity generation. The amount of coal consumption is decreasing overall, but the share of coal used for power generation is steadily rising as the industrial, residential and commercial sectors are using less coal. These sectors respectively represented 5%, 2% and 0.1% of total coal consumption and a total of 2.5 Mt of coal demand in 2010.

Figure 26. **Coal resource areas and infrastructure, 2010**

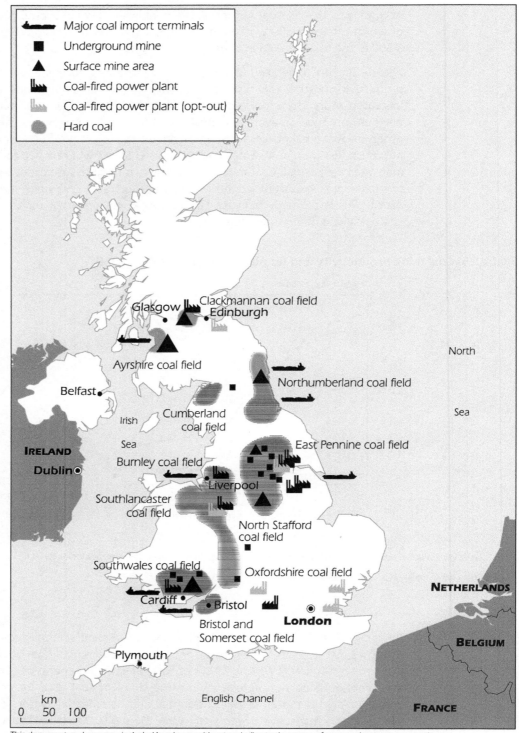

This document and any map included herein are without prejudice to the status of or sovereignty over any territory, to the delimitation of international frontiers and boundaries and to the name of any territory, city or area.

Note: Coal-fired power plants opted out under the EU Large Combustion Plant Directive and the Industrial Emissions Directive (see subsection on Pollution Control). Indicated ports handle about 75% of the United Kingdom's coal imports in 2009.

Sources: EURACOAL; IEA.

Hard coal demand can be divided into steam coal, representing 88%, mainly used for electricity generation, and coking coal, representing 12% of total coal and mainly used in coke ovens and blast furnaces. Hard coal demand has gradually fallen from around 200 Mt in 1960 and has averaged around 60 Mt over the last decade. As a result of the economic crisis and increasing competition from natural gas, coal demand in 2009 was at the lowest since the Industrial Revolution at about 49 Mt. Demand in 2010 reached 51 Mt.

As coal demand is dominated by electricity generation, developments in this sector are key for future demand. The government expects coal demand for electricity generation to drop by 34% to 29 Mt by 2020. Coal demand for electricity generation is likely to decrease in the mid-term as the United Kingdom takes measures to reduce local air pollution and greenhouse-gas emissions.

TRADE

Since 1984, the United Kingdom has been a net importer of coal. Imports have outpaced domestic production since 2003. Russia is the United Kingdom's largest coal supplier providing 37% of total coal imports in 2010. Colombia accounted for 24%, the United States for 17% and Australia for 12%. Around half of the imports in 2010 came through three ports: Immingham, Clyde and Bristol.

Hard coal imports gradually increased from 2.4 Mt in 1978 to a peak of 50.5 Mt in 2006 (Figure 27). From there, they dropped to 26.5 Mt in 2010, as a result of reduced electricity demand during the economic downturn and increasing competition from gas in power generation.

Figure 27. **Hard coal imports by country, 1980 to 2010**

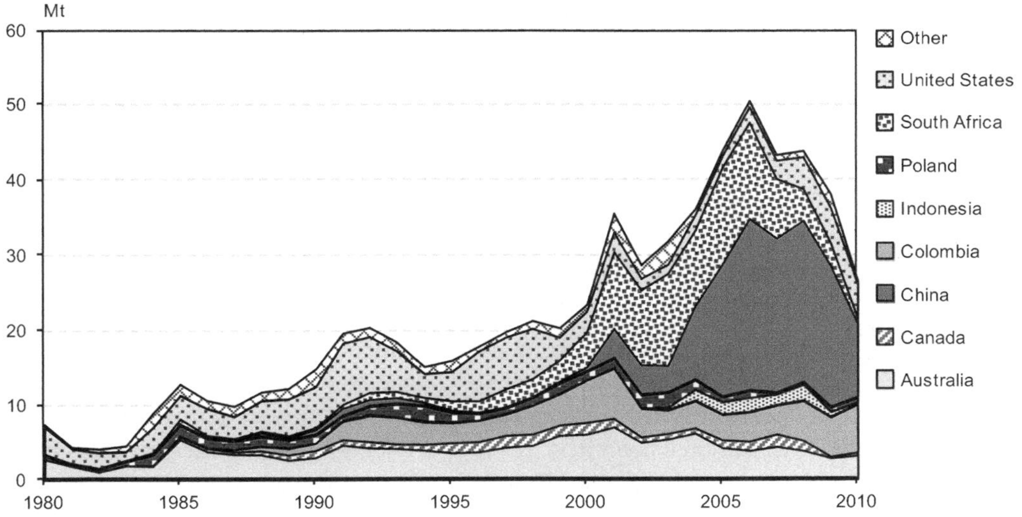

Source: *Coal* Information *2011*, IEA/OECD Paris, 2011.

OUTLOOK

National legislation for carbon emissions and EU air quality directives will affect prospects for the UK coal industry, as both target power generation, which accounts for more than 80% of coal use in the United Kingdom.

The pending electricity market reform (EMR) is also a major factor, and two of the EMR instruments will affect coal demand in particular, namely the carbon price floor (CPF) and the emissions performance standard (EPS). EMR is discussed in more detail in Chapter 10.

The CPF will set a long-term fixed minimum price for carbon dioxide (CO_2) emissions, regardless of the emission allowance price under the EU-ETS. Price for emitting carbon will increase and will penalise coal-fired generation. The EPS, in turn, will cap total annual emissions for fossil fuel power stations at 450 grams of CO_2 per kilowatt-hour (kWh) at baseload. This is stricter than state-of-the-art coal-plant technology can achieve. Therefore, the limit could only be reached by baseload coal plant with the application of carbon capture and storage (CCS) technology.

The United Kingdom's 18 coal-fired power plants have a total installed capacity of around 24 gigawatts (GW) and an average age of about 40 years. Obligations under the EU's Large Combustion Plants Directive (LCPD, 2001/80/EC) will limit the use of 8 GW of this capacity to 20 000 hours until the end of 2015, after which they will close. The introduction of the Industrial Emissions Directive (IED, 2010/75/EU) will likely further reduce the United Kingdom's remaining coal generation capacity by the end of 2023.

These reductions in generating capacity will also reduce the demand for steam coal. This, as well as competition from natural gas and how that develops in coming years, means that it is difficult to assess how the market will develop. Current average coal-plant utilisation rates are well below maximum potential, so a reduction in generating capacity could generally be compensated by higher use of the remaining capacity, but this may not be possible within other operating constraints.

If utilisation rates remain at average levels, steam coal demand could decline from about 42 Mt in 2010 to 36 Mt by the end of 2019. If utilisation rates remain at low 2009/10 levels, coal demand could decline by 14 Mt to around 28 Mt by the end of 2020. This example shows the high variability of coal demand from electricity generation, relative only to different utilisation factors.

Today, domestic production of 18 Mt covers about 38% of steam coal demand. If demand for steam coal is lower, domestic production could cover around 60% of demand from 2021. As the average age of the United Kingdom's coal-fired fleet will be at 47 years by 2020, additional coal capacity may be phased out. Such a development could further reduce domestic coal demand. Finding new markets for coal overseas would be challenging, because of its relatively high price.

To ensure stable domestic production after 2020, new coal mine developments, especially deep mines, need to start permitting procedures and make investments in the near term. Uncertainty related to domestic coal demand after 2020 and unstable export conditions mean that major coal mine investments are on hold. Because of the high costs associated with mothballing a mine – on the order of GBP 0.75 million to GBP 1 million per year for each mine, and subsequently the costs of reopening a deep mine, industries are likely to choose closure of the mines. Therefore, a postponed investment decision today is likely to result in structural losses in the deep mining industry. If coal demand rebounds with the integration of CCS-equipped coal plants, this could increase the United Kingdom's coal import demand.

Surface mines face lower up-front development costs than deep mines. So the effects of uncertainty should be less likely to affect the long-term coal supply contribution from surface mines. However, this sector is vulnerable to uncertainty about levels of future demand which could lead some operators to withdraw from new projects rather than risk exposure to restoration costs for final sites when collapse in demand for coal has left them with inadequate income to meet them.

COAL INDUSTRY POLICY

DECC is in charge of coal industry policy. The UK Coal Authority provides a number of legal, property, planning, environmental and emergency services to members of the public, and to public and private sector organisations. The coal industry has been fully privatised since the 1994 Coal Industry Act.

SUBSIDIES

The selling price of domestic coal in the United Kingdom is freely negotiated. Domestic coal prices are competitive with imports. Since 2002, no state aid is given to support coal mine operating costs and since 2008 none to maintain access to already exploited coal reserves.

From 2004 to 2009, the government subsidised maintaining access to viable reserves at twelve deep mines. The total subsidies amounted to GBP 52.8 million over the five years. They were required to ensure investments under unfavourable global market price conditions.

POLLUTION CONTROL

The Large Combustion Plant Directive (LCPD) aims to reduce acidification, ground level ozone and particulates by controlling the emissions of sulphur dioxide, oxides of nitrogen and dust from large combustion plant. All combustion plants built after 1987 must comply with the LCPD emission limits. Those power stations in operation before 1987 (all coal and oil plants in the United Kingdom) are defined as "existing plant". They have three options for complying: by installing emission abatement equipment, *e.g.* flue-gas desulphurisation; by operating within a "National Plan" setting a national annual mass of emissions calculated by applying the emission limit value (ELV) approach to existing plants, on the basis of those plants' average actual operating hours, fuel used and thermal input, over the five years to 2000; or by opting out of the directive. An existing plant that chooses to opt out is restricted to 20 000 total hours of operation after 2007 and must close by the end of 2015.

In 2011, the Industrial Emissions Directive (IED) came into force, updating and merging seven pieces of existing legislation, including the LCPD. For power plants, the update tightens emission limit values (ELVs) for sulphur dioxide (from 400 mg/Nm^3 to 200 mg/Nm^3). Operators will have to install selective catalytic reduction from 2016 to meet the nitrogen oxides (NO$_x$) ELV. Peaking plants (<1 500 annual operating hours) can run indefinitely, a Transitional National Plan to mid-2020 allows trading in most pollutant categories to achieve emissions reductions equivalent to the directive's ELVs, and a derogation allows operators to run their plants for just 17 500 hours after 1 January 2016 before closure, which must be before the end of 2023.

For the United Kingdom, the LCPD will lead to a closure of 8 GW of coal-fired capacity by the end of 2015, equalling almost 30% of all coal capacity and almost 10% of total installed capacity. The implementation of the IED will affect the remaining capacity. With the phase-out of existing coal plant capacity, coal demand could decrease as well, but also be compensated by increased use of the remaining coal plants.

RESEARCH AND DEVELOPMENT

Coal research, development and demonstration (RD&D) policy in the United Kingdom aims to develop and improve clean coal technologies (CCT) in response to environmental concerns. RD&D efforts in the United Kingdom over the last decades have proven successful and benefited from various aspects of coal preparation, use and technologies for export. For example, the United Kingdom is an exporter of low-NO_x burners, supercritical boilers, flexible plants and life-extending retrofits.

The United Kingdom's policy has focused on specific issues related to the development and implementation of enhanced mining technologies, safety and environmental protection. Under this strategy, the country has successfully developed and implemented measures to handle methane from coal mines. The proper equipment and regulations currently allow for potential exploitation of methane, enhanced mine safety and greenhouse-gas abatement at more than 900 former deep mines. The United Kingdom has also made efforts over the last few years to exploit methane from unworked coal seams (coal-bed methane). Several pilot drilling projects have been completed, but commercial production remains limited. Companies are now using directional drilling techniques, developed in the oil industry, to make coal-bed methane exploitation a viable prospect in the United Kingdom.

Underground coal gasification (UCG) has been of interest on and off in the United Kingdom since the late 1940s. Over that period, the United Kingdom has invested in the development of technology and in a number of test sites, both at home and abroad. The United Kingdom considers that UCG has potential to provide a clean, efficient and convenient source of energy from coal seams where traditional mining methods are not economic. Over many years, in implementing its various UCG development programmes, the United Kingdom has gained widespread knowledge in required drilling methods, environmental and technical implications, as well as in its coal reserves and the economic potential to exploit them. In 2009, the UK Coal Authority awarded the first UCG licence to Thornton New Energy Ltd, a subsidiary of BCG Energy Ltd, in Fife, Scotland. The Coal Authority has granted about 14 conditional near-offshore UCG licences to companies that are keen to pursue the opportunity. However, there is further need for the demonstration and deployment of new extraction processes.

Current coal RD&D activities are undertaken by industry, research institutes and the government, and are managed under the British Coal Utilisation Research Association. The Coal Research Forum provides networking opportunities. Such programmes have already increased and will further increase the environmental acceptability of coal extraction, preparation and use.

According to the Coal Research Forum, the United Kingdom's coal RD&D should focus on efficiency improvements of boilers and turbines, with the advanced supercritical pulverised coal boiler/steam and gas turbine system in the 400 to 1 000 MW_e range as a prime industrial interest. At the same time, economic attractiveness has to be maintained. These improvements should also include: the effective removal of conventional pollutants such as sulphur dioxide, oxides of nitrogen, particulates and trace metals; improved plant integration; operational flexibility; and technologies capable of using a range of coal types appropriate in different global markets. In this regard, the United Kingdom's engagement in several international collaborations is a prerequisite.

Coupled with these current RD&D programmes, coming from a position of international leadership in clean coal technologies, the United Kingdom nowadays is also a front-runner in developing and implementing advanced clean coal technologies such as CCS. The successful market integration of CCS is key to long-term coal use for electricity generation in the United Kingdom. Otherwise, domestic steam coal demand is deemed to be phased out.

CRITIQUE

Coal supplied 15% of primary energy and 29% of electricity generation in 2010. Indigenous coal provides a third of the total and brings security of supply benefits. Risks of potential coal supply disruptions, which would affect electricity supply, can be managed by the balance between domestic production and imported coal. Even though investment to develop deep mine reserves would be economic under current market prices, uncertainty concerning domestic demand levels in the near and medium term is creating an investment barrier. As economically recoverable hard coal reserves accessible from established mines have a relatively short life, and with no prospect of new mines being developed, indigenous hard coal production is likely to decrease considerably after 2020.

Investment decisions and planning consents would be needed in the coming years, if indigenous production is to maintain its current share in meeting coal demand. In light of a potential rebound in coal demand with the widespread deployment of CCS, the challenge is to maintain a skilled workforce for operating coal mines safely.

Coal-fired power generation capacity is expected to decline significantly in the medium term, because of EU air quality legislation, UK climate policy goals and the advanced average age of existing plants. Therefore, diversity in the power sector could decline with other fuels filling potential gaps until CCS for coal becomes a viable option. For energy security purposes, it is essential to maintain the level of energy diversity, both for coal sources and electricity generation sources.

Prospects for the development of clean coal technologies are good. Already reached and ongoing technological improvements mean that a number of innovative pilot projects for methane recovery and underground gasification have been initiated, planned or are under consideration. The development and proven viability for CCS is another pillar for UK coal industry development. The advances so far and the ongoing developments will further contribute to the country's global competitiveness regarding clean coal technologies. This level of knowledge and competitiveness should be maintained and enhanced.

RECOMMENDATIONS

The government of the United Kingdom should:

☐ *Strive to maintain a stable indigenous hard coal production level beyond 2020.*

☐ *Continue with its policy to maintain internationally competitive and innovative clean coal technology development, including coal-related CCS development, demonstration and deployment.*

7. CARBON CAPTURE AND STORAGE

OVERVIEW

The government views carbon capture and storage (CCS) as a critical option in efforts to achieve global greenhouse-gas emissions (GHG) reduction targets. The government recognises that widespread deployment of CCS presents a significant economic opportunity that can build on the considerable existing skill base in the United Kingdom's fossil fuel industry. Consequently, legislative initiatives and financial support schemes have been put in place in recent years to promote the development and deployment of CCS. Yet, while these national, as well as European Union, initiatives have attracted considerable interest from industry, there have been significant challenges that have impeded efforts to move any of the proposed large-scale CCS projects to project realisation.

POLICY, FUNDING AND REGULATORY FRAMEWORK

The main drivers for CCS efforts in the United Kingdom are the national targets to reduce GHG emissions by 50% by 2027 and 80% by 2050 from 1990 levels. The Department of Energy and Climate Change (DECC) estimates that CCS could provide up to 20% of the required carbon dioxide (CO_2) emissions reductions by 2050. The United Kingdom's 2050 Carbon Plan (published in 2011) suggests that 40 gigawatts (GW) of power generating capacity with CCS could be required by 2050. According to the government, CCS technology could also become a significant economic opportunity by using existing skills in fossil-fuel power generation, and in the oil and gas industry. Estimates are that the domestic CCS sector could grow to GBP 3 billion by 2020 and provide export opportunities valued at GBP 6.5 billion per year by 2030.

In order to further support the development and deployment of CCS, the Office of Carbon Capture & Storage was created in 2010 under DECC. It is responsible for developing and co-ordinating CCS activities and a national CCS strategy, including a specific national roadmap to 2050.

CCS deployment will also be influenced by the pending electricity market reform. The July 2011 White Paper on the United Kingdom's future low-carbon electricity sector outlines plans for a new system of long-term contracts in the form of feed-in tariffs with contracts for difference to encourage investments in low-carbon electricity generation, including CCS plants (see Chapter 10).

The electricity market reform, if adopted as in the White Paper, would also entail a CO_2 emissions performance standard at an annual limit equivalent to 450 grams of CO_2 per kilowatt-hour (kWh) of baseload power produced. Thus, new coal-fired power plants would need to be equipped with CCS at least for a proportion of the capacity. Plants in the UK CCS Programme or benefiting from EU funding for commercial-scale CCS would be exempt from the CO_2 emissions performance standard regulations. The White Paper also proposes a carbon price floor of about GBP 16 per tonne of CO_2 in 2013, which will increase to GPB 30 per tonne in 2020 and to GBP 70 per tonne of CO_2 in 2030. The government has committed to providing relief from the carbon price floor for power stations equipped with CCS in proportion to the carbon captured and stored.

In a competition launched in 2007, the government pledged up to GBP 1 billion for the CCS-related expenses of the first domestic commercial-scale CCS demonstration in power generation. It was to have been awarded in 2011. However, by October 2011, all of the CCS projects in the competition were cancelled. Among them was the CCS project at Longannet, which had been considered one of the most advanced projects on a global scale as well as being the last participant in the competition.

In 2011, DECC submitted applications for seven CCS projects for EU funding. The government remains committed to enabling cost-competitive deployment of CCS in the 2020s. There are a number of promising projects in the United Kingdom and a new accelerated selection process will be launched in spring 2012. The government has also introduced a range of legislative measures to enable CCS demonstration and deployment, and transposed the EU Directive on the Geological Storage of Carbon Dioxide (2009/31/EC).[8] Specific legislation for regulating the environmental impact of long-term storage of CO_2 was implemented in the Energy Act of 2008 and subsequently adapted as part of transposing the EU CCS Directive. As required by that directive, the government has also introduced detailed specifications for assessing the technical and economic feasibility of retrofitting future combustion power plants larger than 300 MW with CCS. With respect to international regulations, the ratification of a recent CCS amendment to the London Protocol is complete. Ratification by the United Kingdom and other London Protocol parties is necessary to allow transboundary export of CO_2 for injection into sub-seabed geological formations.

INTERNATIONAL ENGAGEMENT

The United Kingdom participates in many international forums and has several CCS partnerships. These include high-level multilateral initiatives, such as the Carbon Sequestration Leadership Forum (CSLF), an international ministerial-level initiative for promoting CCS. The government hosted the CSLF Ministerial Meeting in London in 2009. Jointly with Australia, the United Kingdom is leading the Carbon Capture, Use and Storage Action Group on how to overcome key barriers to CCS deployment. The Action Group was established at the Clean Energy Ministerial in Washington D.C. in 2010.

These activities are supplemented by a variety of bilateral, multilateral and regional CCS activities, including:

- Under a Memorandum of Understanding (MoU), DECC is fostering academic and industrial collaboration on energy research, development and demonstration (RD&D) between the United Kingdom and the United States, with increasing attention on CCS.

- Jointly with Norway, the United Kingdom established the North Sea Basin Task Force in 2005 in order to develop common principles for managing and regulating the transport, injection and permanent storage of CO_2 in the North Sea sub-seabed.

---

8. Additional details on legal and regulatory developments are summarised regularly in the IEA *Carbon Capture and Storage Legal and Regulatory Review* (http://www.iea.org/Papers/2011/ccs_legal.pdf).

In May 2009, the two countries started to evaluate opportunities for CO_2 storage under the seabed as part of their "One North Sea" initiative.

- Seeing potential for fruitful collaboration between oil-producing nations committed to advancing CCS development and deployment, the "Four Kingdoms" CCS Initiative was established in 2008 between the United Kingdom, Norway, the Netherlands and Saudi Arabia. Its purpose is to identify and address technical issues, including gaps in knowledge, which could impede commercialisation of CCS, to act in a co-ordinated manner to enhance national expertise on CCS and to encourage the sharing of knowledge and the transfer of technology.

- The United Kingdom and the European Union signed MoUs with the Chinese Ministry of Science and Technology (MOST) in 2005 that led to the Near Zero Emissions Coal (NZEC) Initiative and Co-operation Action within CCS China (COACH) projects. Both projects examined options for CCS in China (COACH focused specifically on integrated gasification combined cycle technology) and examined storage potential in the north-east region of China.

- DECC has also co-funded other international engagement activities, such as the National Centre for Carbon Capture and Storage in South Africa, and capacity-building projects for CCS in India and Indonesia.

PROJECTS AND RESEARCH

PILOT AND RESEARCH ACTIVITIES

The United Kingdom has several CO_2 capture pilot plants for testing and optimisation purposes. Some of these projects have now ended, others are just beginning operations. These include:

- The Ferrybridge CC100+ project: This is the largest post combustion capture plant in the United Kingdom. It was launched in November 2011 at SSE's Ferrybridge coal-fired power station in West Yorkshire and will begin a two-test programme in January 2012. This is a 5 MW_e pilot project which will capture up to 100 tonnes of CO_2 (tCO_2) per day using amine-based post-combustion capture technology supplied by Doosan Babcock on the flue-gas from the power station. The government has invested more than GBP 6 million in this GBP 20 million project with partners SSE, Doosan Power Systems and Vattenfall.

- Doosan Babcock's 40 MW oxyfuel (Oxycoal 2) combustion pilot project at their Clean Combustion Test Facility in Renfrew, Scotland. The project, a test rig adapted specifically for testing oxyfuel capture technology on pulverised coal and applicable to both new and retrofitted supercritical boilers, completed the test programme in early 2011. The project involved a number of partners from industry and academia and received a UK government grant.

- Aberthaw carbon capture plant: This privately funded 3 MW_e pilot project will test amine post-combustion capture technology supplied by Cansolv on RWE nPower's Aberthaw coal-fired power station in Wales. It will capture around 50 tCO_2 per day. The plant is expected to become operational in 2012. RWE nPower has also been operating CO_2 capture test facilities for post-combustion and oxyfuel capture at their Didcot power station since 2008.

The United Kingdom has also been involved with a number of carbon storage projects. These include:

- UK CO_2 Storage Appraisal Project (UKSDAP): This GBP 4 million project was set up in October 2009 by the United Kingdom's Energy Technology Institute (ETI) which receives 50% of its funding from the government. The project reviewed UK offshore CO_2 storage sites and storage estimates. This project has now completed and results will be available later in 2012 through a web-enabled database and GIS.

- CO_2ReMoVe (research, monitoring and verification): The United Kingdom has been involved in this EU Framework Programme project set up in 2006 to research, develop and test monitoring techniques for CO_2 geological storage at real, industrial-scale storage sites. The project will complete at the end of March 2012. The United Kingdom provided funding to Quintessa, a UK consultancy company to develop a database (CO_2 FEP) which models and assesses performance and safety of storage sites as part of the wider project.

In addition to industrial activities, several academic institutions are engaged in CCS research. These include the universities of Cranfield, Edinburgh, Leeds, Newcastle, Nottingham, Sheffield and the Imperial College London. Between 2011 and 2015, the government expects to invest GBP 125 million in fundamental and applied research related to CCS through several organisations, including DECC, the Research Councils, the Technology Strategy Board, and the Energy Technologies Institute.

DEMONSTRATION PROJECTS

In terms of large-scale CCS demonstration, the Longannet CCS project was the only remaining bid under the government's CCS competition for the first commercial-scale CCS plant in the United Kingdom. However, plans for the plant were scrapped in October 2011 after a front-end engineering study was completed. The project consortium concluded that the project would not be commercially viable without public funding in addition to the GBP 1 billion from the government. The Longannet power station, with a capacity of 2 400 MW, is located on the east coast of Scotland. The proposal was to demonstrate post-combustion CO_2 capture with amines by retrofitting 330 MW of the plant with CCS.

Other CCS demonstration plants in the United Kingdom have been proposed, but their feasibility assessments and plans have not progressed to the level of the Longannet project. Therefore, its cancellation is a major setback and will lead to significant delays in putting the first large-scale CCS demonstration in the United Kingdom on the ground. A delay of at least a year is expected at another planned large CCS project at a new coal-fired plant at Hunterston in Ayrshire because of a record number of formal objections by organisations and individuals. Nevertheless, other proposed CCS projects have announced intentions to accelerate development of front-end engineering and design studies to gain position in the competition for the pledged government funding. The most promising candidates are the six CCS projects remaining after the cancellation of Longannet that have submitted applications to the European Investment Bank (EIB) for consideration in the next round of the EU's New Entrants Reserve (NER) scheme. Funding decisions are expected in the second half of 2012. The NER call supports CCS and renewable energy projects with up to three projects per EU member state. Proposals from the United Kingdom include CCS projects for:

- Alstom Limited Consortium: oxyfuel new supercritical coal-fired power station at the Drax site in north Yorkshire;

- C.GEN: new integrated gasification combined cycle (IGCC) power station (pre-combustion with CCS on the coal-feed) in Killingholme, Yorkshire;

- Peel Energy CCS Ltd: post-combustion amine capture on new supercritical coal-fired power station in Ayrshire, Scotland;

- Don Valley Power Project (formerly known as the Hatfield Project): new IGCC power station in Stainforth, Yorkshire;

- A consortium led by Progressive Energy Ltd: pre-combustion coal gasification project in Teesside, north-east England; and

- SSE Generation Ltd: post-combustion capture retrofitted to an existing combined-cycle gas turbine power station at Peterhead, Scotland.

CO_2 STORAGE POTENTIAL

As is the case in most of the world, the theoretical and economic potential for CO_2 storage in the United Kingdom is uncertain. Significant research is under way to improve capacity estimates. The work is focusing on offshore storage in deep saline aquifers, and depleted oil and natural gas fields. The European GeoCapacity Project report in 2009 estimates a range of total theoretical CO_2 storage capacity in the United Kingdom at about 14 gigatonnes (Gt) under conservative assumptions to 25 Gt under more optimistic assumptions.

CO_2 emissions from large point sources, such as coal-fired power plants, are assumed to be particularly attractive for CCS storage applications because of expected economies of scale. According to the European GeoCapacity study, these emissions averaged 0.26 Gt per year in the United Kingdom from 2003 to 2005. For comparison, total UK CO_2 emissions in 2005 were 0.6 Gt. CO_2 could also be stored in association with enhanced oil recovery. A 2009 study by the IEA Greenhouse Gas R&D Programme estimates storage potential of 4 Gt from enhanced oil recovery in the United Kingdom fields in the North Sea Graben Basin.[9]

CRITIQUE

The government has demonstrated strong commitment to support widespread deployment of CCS technology. CCS is considered a vital technology for meeting both the national GHG target by 2025 and the legally binding CO_2 reduction obligations by 2050. The government has dedicated significant resources to CCS and initiated a variety of regulatory and incentive mechanisms to accelerate CCS development and demonstration. This includes the commitment to support the first national commercial-scale demonstration plant with up to GBP 1 billion, which likely is the largest fund allocated to a single CCS plant worldwide. Despite comparably strong interest from UK industry to engage in national and EU CCS demonstration project competitions, industry and government have struggled to advance any of the proposed CCS projects close to a firm investment decision.

---

9. www.ieaghg.org

The Longannet CCS project was the last participant in a four-year competition for the GBP 1 billion in public support for the first large-scale CCS demonstration. Its cancellation in October 2011 marks a major setback in CCS development and in the government's ambition to make the United Kingdom a global front-runner in CCS deployment. Since alternative project proposals are in a much less mature development state, large-scale CCS demonstration will be delayed. It remains to be seen to what extent this development will also impact other activities, such as the forthcoming competition to select projects for support. Considering the long time required for permitting and constructing CCS plants, the regulatory framework will need to be detailed very soon.

Given the required time from planning to operation, the government should now focus on the most developed CCS project proposals. When front-end engineering and design studies are complete, priority should be given to identify which project qualifies for the GBP 1 billion in financial support in order to advance the first large-scale demonstration project. In parallel, momentum should be maintained to further analyse the required CCS infrastructure development, covering optimal site selection and co-ordination of capture, transport and storage of CO_2 at various facilities. By using an integrated approach, regional clusters could be supported to use common infrastructure that would help reduce project costs. Cost-optimised integrated infrastructure planning should address CCS-related aspects and be co-ordinated with infrastructure requirements of present and future electricity generation, transmission and fuel transport needs.

The CO_2 emissions performance standard proposed as part of the electricity market reform is a clear statement by the government not to allow any new coal-fired power plants without CCS. Given the expected strong role for natural gas-fired power generation in the next decade, and the potential role that gas with CCS could play, it is an important signal by the government to explicitly include applications for demonstrating CCS at gas-fired power stations. In case even the large funding pledge by the government for the first CCS project should turn out to be insufficient to attract a commercial-scale CCS project at a coal plant, it would be worthwhile considering whether a CCS technology demonstration at a gas-fired power station would be a viable option.

The United Kingdom has been quite engaged in implementing appropriate CCS-related legal and regulatory frameworks. In addition, the pending electricity market reform could stimulate broader deployment of CCS technology and, along with a successful large-scale demonstration, will underscore the government's interest in effective CCS technology development.

The government is globally among the most committed supporters of the development and deployment of CCS. Apart from putting aside a very large fund for CCS demonstration, support to research activities has helped domestic universities to become some of the most active academic institutions on CCS worldwide. The United Kingdom has also significantly engaged in global collaboration and knowledge exchange with leading developed and developing countries. This includes assuming a leading role in key CCS-related ministerial-level initiatives, such as the Carbon Capture, Use and Storage Action Group. Given the importance of CCS for addressing climate change and as a key economic opportunity for industry, the government should keep up its very high engagement in promoting CCS.

RECOMMENDATIONS

The government of the United Kingdom should:

☐ *Maintain strong financial and political engagement in supporting four CCS demonstration plants, despite a challenging financial context; maintain a leading position in global collaboration and capacity building on CCS.*

☐ *Analyse the reasons for the lack of success in the competition for financing the first large-scale CCS project; accelerate and support the development of alternative large-scale demonstration projects.*

☐ *Adopt legal and regulatory frameworks required for CCS, in particular related to sub-seabed storage and cross-border transportation.*

☐ *Continue to develop a long-term policy vision and a national roadmap for CCS; continue long-term CCS infrastructure planning, while taking into account the broader infrastructure requirements of power generation, transmission and fuel transportation.*

8. RENEWABLE ENERGY

Key data (2010)

Share of renewable energy: 3.7% of total primary energy supply (TPES) and 7.2% of electricity generation (IEA averages: 7.7% of TPES and 17.7% of electricity generation)

Biofuels and waste: 2.9% of TPES and 3.5% of electricity generation

Wind power: 0.4% of TPES and 2.7% of total electricity generation

Other renewable energy: 0.2% of TPES and 1% of electricity generation

SUPPLY AND DEMAND

SUPPLY

The share of renewable energy in the United Kingdom's total primary energy supply (TPES) has increased significantly in recent years, from 1.5% in 2003 to 3.7% (7.2 million tonnes of oil equivalent) in 2010 (see Figure 28). Yet, the United Kingdom ranks fourth-lowest among IEA member countries (see Figure 29).

Biofuels and waste were the largest renewable energy sources in the United Kingdom, at 5.9 Mtoe, 2.9% of TPES in 2010. Biofuels and waste can be broken down into primary solid biofuels (34%), biogases (30%), liquid biofuels (19%) and industrial and municipal wastes (17%). The share of biogases is particularly high compared to most IEA countries; biogas contributes nearly 1% of TPES, while the IEA average is about 0.3%. Only Germany has a higher share with biogases accounting for 1.5% of TPES. In the United Kingdom, 21% of total biofuels and waste are imported (17% of primary solid biofuels and 81% of liquid biodiesel).

The second most important renewable source is wind energy, accounting for 0.4% of TPES in 2010. The amount of energy generated from wind has increased almost fourfold in five years and is expected to continue on its steep growth trend until 2020.

Other renewable energy sources made a negligible contribution to the total energy mix: hydropower represented 0.2% of TPES and solar energy 0.04% in 2010. The government estimates that renewable energy supply could increase to 16.6% of TPES in 2020, partly compensating the decreasing supply of fossil fuels and nuclear. Biofuels and waste are estimated to increase to 22 Mtoe, 13% of TPES in the decade, and wind power to reach 4% of TPES. For comparison, wind provided 3.4% of energy supply in Denmark in 2010, the highest wind share in TPES among IEA countries.

Figure 28. **Renewable energy in total primary energy supply in the United Kingdom, 1980 to 2020**

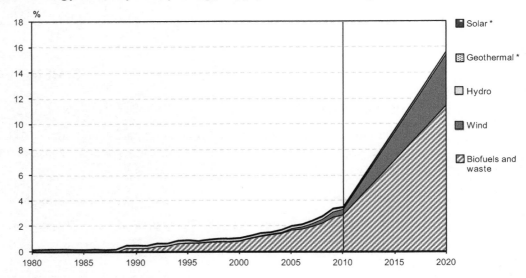

* Negligible.

Note: This graph shows historical data to 2010 and government projections for 2011 to 2020.

Sources: *Energy Balances of OECD Countries*, IEA/OECD Paris, 2011 and country submission.

Figure 29. **Renewable energy in total primary energy supply in IEA countries, 2010***

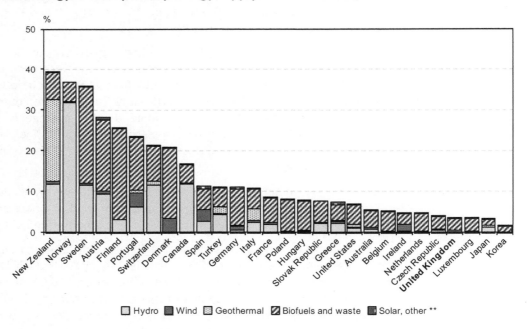

* Estimates.

** *Other* includes tidal, wave and ambient heat used in heat pumps.

Source: *Energy Balances of OECD Countries*, IEA/OECD Paris, 2011.

ELECTRICITY GENERATION

Renewable energy sources represented 7.2% of total electricity generation in the United Kingdom in 2010, up from 2.8% in 2000 (see Figure 30). Biogases, waste and most solid biofuels are used for electricity and heat generation; this represents two-thirds of total biofuels and waste, generating 13 terawatt-hours (TWh) or 3.5% of total electricity in 2010. In addition, 10 TWh were generated from wind energy, accounting for 2.7% of total electricity generation and 3.6 TWh from hydro.

Figure 30. **Electricity generation from renewable energy in the United Kingdom, 1980 to 2020**

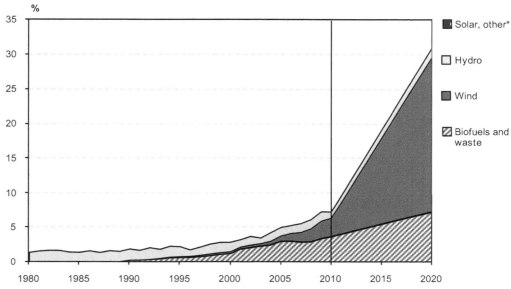

* Negligible.

Note: This graph shows historical data to 2010 and government projections for 2011 to 2020.

Sources: *Energy Balances of OECD Countries*, IEA/OECD Paris, 2011 and country submission.

Wind has had the strongest growth and is expected to continue its exponential trend until 2020. The government expects wind to generate around 75 TWh in 2020, representing around 20% of total electricity generation. The United Kingdom is the global leader in offshore wind power with 1.3 gigawatt (GW) of capacity in fifteen wind farms, which generated 3 TWh in 2010. By early 2012, offshore wind capacity in the United Kingdom had increased to nearly 2 GW. RenewableUK, an industry body, expects offshore wind capacity to increase to 8 GW by 2016 and to 18 GW by 2020.

Compared to other IEA countries, electricity generation from renewable energy sources is rather low in the United Kingdom. As with TPES, it is the third-lowest share among IEA countries, ahead only of the Czech Republic and Korea (Figure 31).

Figure 31. **Renewables in total electricity generation in IEA countries, 2010***

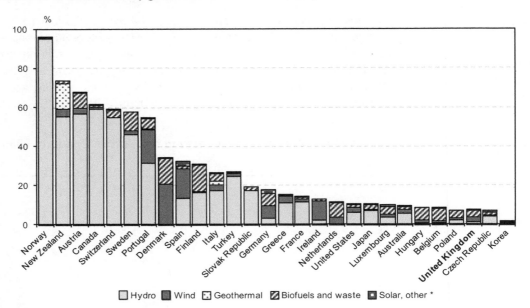

* Estimates.

** *Other* includes ambient heat used in heat pumps.

Source: *Energy Balances of OECD Countries*, IEA/OECD Paris, 2011.

INSTITUTIONS

The **Department of Energy and Climate Change** (DECC), established in October 2008, has the lead on renewable electricity and heat within the UK government. Within DECC, the *Office of Renewable Energy Deployment* (ORED) ensures that targets to deploy renewable energy are met. DECC works closely with the regulatory body that oversees the operation of the electricity market, the **Office of Gas and Electricity Markets** (Ofgem), and **National Grid** which owns and operates the high-voltage transmission system in England and Wales and also operates the Scottish system. The **Department of Transport** has responsibility for renewable energy initiatives in the transport sector.

The **Marine Management Organisation** was established in 2010 under the Marine and Coastal Access Act to oversee deployment of offshore energy installations of less than 100 megawatts (MW) in English waters.

POLICIES AND MEASURES

European Union (EU) Directive 2009/28/EC requires each EU member state to increase the share of renewable energy in its gross final consumption. The directive targets an overall EU renewables share of 20% in 2020. It also targets a 10% renewable energy share in transport. Under the directive, the United Kingdom is to achieve at least a 15% renewable energy share by 2020.

In 2010, renewable energy met 3.3% (54 TWh) of gross total final consumption (TFC). A more than fourfold increase is needed to meet the 2020 target, representing an average increase of 17% per year.

While the 15% renewables target is binding, the manner in which an individual member state achieves it is at its discretion. The directive obliges member states to develop a National Renewable Energy Action Plan (NREAP). The United Kingdom published its NREAP in July 2010. This plan translated the 15% energy target to 238 TWh, based on energy demand projections for 2020. The ongoing Renewables Obligation Banding Review, which is reassessing the rates of support to specific renewable energy technologies under the Renewables Obligation, suggests that 108 TWh of this should be generated by large-scale projects, with the remainder from small-scale ones, renewable heat and renewable transport fuels.

Devolved administrations within the United Kingdom have elected to go beyond these targets. For example, the Scottish government has chosen to pursue 30% of energy consumption from renewable energy sources by 2020.

The recent Renewable Energy Review, conducted by the Committee on Climate Change for the government and published in May 2011, concluded that renewable energy could cover 30% to 45% of all UK energy requirements by 2030. Subsequently, DECC published its Renewable Energy Roadmap, which makes an approximation of the proportions of different renewable energy technologies needed to reach the 2020 target (see Figure 32).

Figure 32. **UK renewable energy roadmap: technology contributions in the central scenario, 2020**

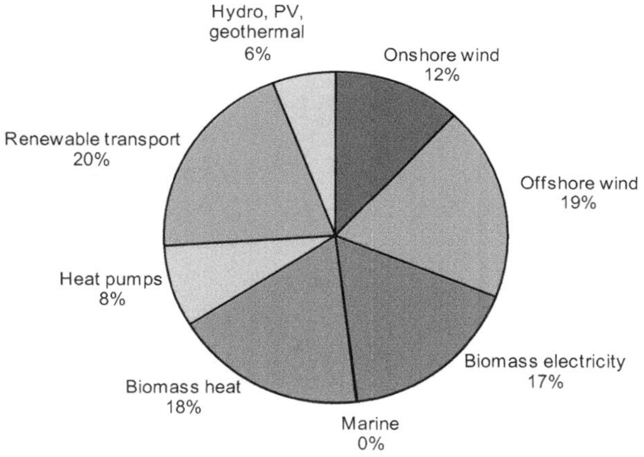

Source: UK Renewable Energy Roadmap, DECC, 2011.

The DECC roadmap focuses on removing non-economic barriers to renewable energy, centring on a number of key actions:

- Providing grid access to the backlog of 5.5 GW of consented projects waiting for a grid connection. An offshore grid is also targeted to provide for wind and marine energy technology deployment.

- Reducing investor risk through the maintenance of stable long-term support for renewables in the face of reform of the Renewables Obligation, the establishment of a replacement/parallel support model based on feed-in tariffs (for large-scale projects) and other scheduled reforms of the electricity market.[10]

---

10. Feed-in tariffs are already used to support small-scale projects.

- Reducing planning delays, including a radar replacement programme and the replacement of the present Infrastructure Planning Commission with a Major Infrastructure Planning Unit.

- Strengthening bioenergy feedstock supply chains, while putting in place sustainability standards, and a bioenergy strategy to optimise use of the existing resources.

- Removing constraints on supply chains for equipment, installers and infrastructure. Tasks include port and manufacturing facilities for offshore wind, marine energy parks and charging infrastructure for plug-in electric vehicles.

- Funding innovation to support advances in offshore and marine technologies, as well as possible support for energy-from-waste and biomass.

DECC published a Biomass Strategy in May 2007, which targets the increase of biomass use in the electricity, heat and transport sectors, and considers opportunities to increase domestic supply to 96.2 TWh or 8.3 Mtoe. DECC estimates that bioenergy could contribute up to half of the country's 2020 renewable energy targets. Options include:

- an additional 1 million dry tonnes of wood annually from unmanaged woodlands;

- increased recovery of waste wood from managed woodlands and other sources;

- increased energy cropping by 350 000 hectares across the United Kingdom by 2020 (to 17% of total UK arable land); and

- increased fuel stock provision from organic waste streams.

Currently, the strategy is under review, focusing on the availability of feedstocks to 2020, economic and carbon impacts of using biomass in different energy sectors, as well as outside the energy sector. The review is expected to be complete early in 2012, when a new Bioenergy Strategy will be released.

POLICIES BY SECTOR

Electricity

The National Renewable Energy Action Plan targets 31% of electricity from renewables by 2020, of which 2% is to come from small-scale projects. The Northern Ireland Executive has elected to go further with a target to deliver 40% renewable electricity, while the Scottish government is pursuing 100%.

According to the DECC roadmap, a growth rate of about 15% per year from the 2010 baseline of 28 TWh will be needed to reach the 2020 goal. Encouragingly in 2011, large-scale renewable electricity projects in the pipeline amount to 22 GW, including 11 GW of onshore wind and 4.3 GW of biomass.

Since 2002, the principal renewable energy policy measure in the electricity sector has been the Renewables Obligation (RO), which is administered by the Gas and Electricity Markets Authority (GEMA) through Ofgem. The RO obliges suppliers to source an annually increasing proportion of their electricity from renewable energy sources. The obligation for the 2010/11 period was 11.1%.

Proof of compliance with the quota is ensured via Renewables Obligation Certificates (ROCs), which are issued by Ofgem to renewable electricity generators. These are bundled with the underlying electricity sold to suppliers. If under the quota, suppliers can also buy ROCs from qualified electricity on the open market. Failure by suppliers to present sufficient certificates for the period incurs a penalty: payment of an inflation-adjusted buy-out price (GBP 36.99/MWh in 2010/11). This goes into a buy-out fund, whose revenues are recycled to suppliers in proportion to the number of ROCs submitted. Cost of compliance with the RO is passed onto the consumer. Ofgem estimates that the RO adds around GBP 10 per year to a consumer's electricity bill.

When launched, the RO was technology-neutral, which is to say that one ROC was issued to all renewable electricity generators for each megawatt-hour produced, regardless of which resource underlay that production. In April 2009, technology banding was introduced to reflect differing needs for support and to ensure sufficient returns from less developed technologies so as to encourage their further development. For example, generation from offshore wind projects now receives greater support than cheaper options such as landfill gas (see Table 9).

The NREAP mentions plans to review the RO and Renewable Transport Fuels Obligation, and raises the possibility of a move to a feed-in tariff (FiT) scheme for new large-scale electricity projects. Discussions on the design of this FiT are ongoing, with a proposal for a long-term "contracts for difference" (CfD) model. The final model is expected to be launched in 2014. Under the FiT CfD model, generators would receive the wholesale electricity price, topped up to a contracted level; while, if prices rise above this level, the difference would be reimbursed. Initially, generators would have a one-off choice to opt for the FiT CfD or the RO, but the latter would be retired on 31 March 2017.

Table 9. **Existing and proposed technology bands for Renewables Obligation Certificate eligibility**

Technology band	Present ROC per MWh	Proposed ROC per MWh
Coal plants transformed to biomass	1.5	1 from 2013
Co-firing with biomass (15% +)	0.5	1 from 2013
Co-firing of energy crops	1 (1.5 for CHP)	no change
Dedicated biomass	1.5	1.4 from 2016
Dedicated energy crops	2	1.9 in 2015 1.8 in 2016
Hydroelectricity	1	0.5 from 2013
Combined heat and power using waste	1	0.5 from 2013
Landfill gas	0.25	0 from 2013
Onshore wind	1	0.9 from 2013
Offshore wind	2	1.9 in 2015 1.8 in 2016
Solar PV	2	1.9 in 2015 1.8 in 2016
Large tidal	2	1.9 in 2015 1.8 in 2016
Tidal stream/wave	2	<30 MW: 5 >30 MW: 2

Sources: Consultation on proposals for the levels of banded support under the Renewables Obligation for 2013-2017 and the Renewables Obligation Order 2012.

The Renewables Obligation technology banding levels in England and Wales are under review as detailed above. New levels have been proposed for 2013 to 2017 (and from 2014 for offshore wind). The intention of the review is to reduce levels of support for technologies whose costs have fallen sharply in recent years and to boost support for fledgling technologies, particularly tidal and wave power.

As of April 2010, deployment of small-scale solar PV, wind, hydropower and anaerobic digestion (up to 5 MW) and micro-combined heat and power of up to 2 kW$_e$ has been supported under the feed-in tariffs (FiTs) scheme. The scheme provides a fixed payment per MWh for a period of 10, 20 or 25 years, depending on the technology, and is intended to encourage uptake by households, communities and small businesses in Great Britain.

In August 2011, following a significant fall in solar PV costs and higher than expected response, tariff levels for new PV installations of above 50 kW were sharply reduced. Current generation tariffs for solar PV are: 19 pence per kilowatt-hour (p/kWh) for installations over 50 kW and up to 150 kW; 15 p/kWh for installations over 150 kW and up to 250 kW; and 8.5 p/kWh for installations over 250 kW up to 5 MW. A second phase of the tariff reform, focusing on all scales of solar PV projects under 50 kW, is due to alter tariffs from April 2012. This change includes a sharp tariff reduction for installations below 50 kW.

Planning aspects

Meeting the 2020 renewables targets will require considerable infrastructure development. In part to address this, the Planning Act of 2008 defined nationally significant infrastructure projects (over 50 MW on land and 100 MW offshore), which fall under the remit of an Infrastructure Planning Commission (IPC).[11] The IPC controls these developments on the basis of National Policy Statements designated by DECC and agreed in July 2011.

Under the Localism Act, the IPC will be replaced by a Major Infrastructure Planning Unit (MIPU), within a planning inspectorate. Although one objective of the Act is to increase local involvement in and benefit from infrastructure developments, the MIPU aims to ensure that decision making for strategically important projects such as large power plants and new transmission lines will remain on a fast track.

One measure within the bill is to allow local councils to retain their business rates, rather than these being pooled for national redistribution (as at present). This could provide additional incentives for local communities to accept renewable energy and other projects.

Radar interference concerns relating to large wind power projects have been allayed. The result is that blocked capacity additions have now moved into the construction phase.

Transmission aspects

Before May 2009, the connection of electricity generators to the grid was done with an "invest then connect" approach. In this model, new generators would be connected on a first-come first-served basis and had to wait until any necessary reinforcement to support their connection had been completed.

---

11. A marine planning system was introduced under the Marine and Coastal Access Act of 2009. The Marine (Scotland) Act of 2010 applies in Scottish waters.

Since that date, Ofgem has adopted a "connect and manage" approach. This model, initially for an interim period, means that generators can connect as soon as the local grid connection is established, without waiting for wider reinforcement to take place. This has, as anticipated, resulted in accelerated connection of projects.

Nevertheless, investment in grid reinforcement and extension is urgently needed. A March 2009 report from the Electricity Networks Strategy Group (ENSG), chaired by DECC and Ofgem, stated that additional investments of GBP 4.7 billion in the transmission grid are needed to meet the 2020 renewable energy objectives. This amounts to some 15% of the total transmission investment needed (GBP 32 billion).[12] The investment rate will have to roughly double to achieve this level, relative to the preceding 20 years.

Through Project Transmit, Ofgem is currently reviewing the transmission connection and charging regime to establish whether it provides a sufficiently strong signal to attract needed investment. Among other aspects, the project will assess the benefits of locational electricity pricing to reflect the need for reinforcement in key weak spots.

Central among the investment challenges are the growing proportion of distributed generation, the need to extend the high-voltage grid to renewable resource-rich locations including the offshore, the ability of the system to manage greater supply-side variability and growing electricity demand owing to electrification in the heat and transport sectors. Ofgem has introduced the RIIO regulation (Revenue = Incentives + Innovation + Outputs), which sets price controls, to help meet these challenges at least cost to the consumer.

The Crown Estate estimates that GBP 10 billion will be needed to connect all "Round 3" wind power offshore projects. Offshore transmission development revolves around competitive tenders for licences, under which applicants compete to deliver services at least cost. Successful applicants become offshore transmission owners/operators of a set of transmission assets (which are built by the wind farm developer), with specific obligations, incentives and entitlements. The first offshore transmission operation (OFTO) licence was awarded in April 2011; for the second round, Ofgem anticipated announcing preferred bidders for Tranche A projects in 2012.

The Electricity Networks Strategy Group (ENSG) has proposed offshore high-voltage direct current (HVDC) transmission lines, known as "bootstraps", to reinforce existing links between Scotland and England; and the Offshore Transmission Co-ordination Project is considering the possibility that offshore transmission assets could be used to avoid onshore reinforcements (see subsection on transmission and distribution in Chapter 10).

Heating and cooling

The UK NREAP targets a renewable share in total heat consumption of 12% by 2020. It targets 3 914 kilotonnes of oil equivalent (ktoe) from biomass, 2 254 ktoe from heat pumps and 34 ktoe from solar. The DECC roadmap, which targets 73 TWh by 2020 (from 13 TWh in 2010) suggests that a growth rate of over 19% per year will be needed.

---

12. See www.orgem.gov.uk/Media/FactSheets/Documents1/re-wiringbritainfs.pdf.

A renewable heat premium payment (RHPP), administered by the Energy Saving Trust, has been in place since 1 August 2011 and will run until 31 March 2012. It consists of grants for domestic heat consumers to help in the installation costs of solar water heaters, heat pumps (air/water/ground-sourced) and biomass boilers. Grants range from GBP 300 to GBP 1 250. Total funding amounts to GBP 15 million.

In this sense, the RHPP is the precursor to the Renewable Heat Incentive (RHI) scheme, which was proposed in the NREAP and opened for applications in late November 2011. This followed some delay resulting from the need to adjust the tariff for large biomass-fired facilities to comply with European state aid rules.

But the RHI is a far broader instrument, targeting the full range of heat technologies and applications at all scales. The first priority is large emitters in the industrial, public service, commercial and district heating sectors, which together contribute some 38% of CO_2 emissions. The RHI is administered by Ofgem, which is currently considering the design and timing of phase two of the scheme, which will also include domestic consumers. The government expects RHI to reduce carbon emissions by a total of 44 Mt by 2020, equalling the annual carbon emissions of 20 new CCGTs.

Eligible technologies include biomass, solar thermal, water and ground-source heat pumps, on-site biogas combustion, deep geothermal systems, energy from waste, biomethane injected into the gas grid and renewables-based CHP. Only technologies with an existing commercial track record are eligible: the RHI does not target innovations.

Table 10. **Technologies and tariffs under the Renewable Heat Incentive**

Levels of support				
	Eligible technology	**Eligible sizes**	**Tariff rate** (pence/kWh)	**Support calculation**
Small biomass	Solid biomass; municipal solid waste (including CHP)	Less than 200 kW$_{th}$	Tier 1: **7.6**	Metering. Tier 1 applies annually up to the tier break, Tier 2 above the tier break. The tier break is: installed capacity x 1 314 peak load hours, *i.e.* kW$_{th}$ x 1 314
			Tier 2: **1.9**	
Medium biomass		200 kW$_{th}$ and above; less than 1 000 kW$_{th}$	Tier 1: **4.7**	
			Tier 2: **1.9**	
Large biomass		1 000 kW$_{th}$ and above	**1.0**	Metering
Small ground source	Ground-source heat pumps; water-source heat pumps; deep geothermal	Less than 100 kW$_{th}$	**4.3**	Metering
Large ground source		100 kW$_{th}$ and above	**3**	
Solar thermal	Solar thermal	Less than 200 kW$_{th}$	**8.5**	Metering
Biomethane	Biomethane injection and biogas combustion, except from landfill gas	Biomethane all scales, biogas combustion less than 200 kW$_{th}$	**6.5**	Metering

Note: kW$_{th}$ = kilowatt thermal.

Source: Adapted from Renewable Heat Incentive, DECC, March 2011. Available at: www.decc.gov.uk/assets/decc/What%20we%20do/UK%20energy%20supply/Energy%20mix/Renewable%20energy/policy/renewableheat/1387-renewable-heat-incentive.pdf.

A number of technologies may be considered for eligibility at a later stage, including air-source heat pumps, bioliquids and direct air heating. Bioliquids, as with biofuels, will be subject to sustainability criteria, as well as ongoing evaluation of the costs and benefits of their use in the heat sector relative to other energy and non-energy end-use. Table 10 lists the tariffs available for technologies included in the first phase of the RHI. All incentives run for a period of 20 years.

Other recent support to the renewable heat sector targets includes the Low Carbon Buildings Programme, the Bio-Energy Capital Grants Scheme (BECGS) and the Bioenergy Infrastructure Scheme. The Low Carbon Buildings Programme, which ran from 2006 to 2010, consisted of grants for micro-heat systems amounting to about GBP 131 million for around 20 000 projects.

The BECGS began in 2002, and the sixth round closed in April 2010. It provided capital grants to all sizes of biomass-fuelled heat and CHP plants in England. The level of the grant was 40% of the additional capital costs compared to a fossil fuel alternative.

From 2004, the Bioenergy Infrastructure Scheme supported the biomass supply chain for electricity, heat and CHP producers. The most recent round, its third, closed in February 2010. It targeted small and medium-sized producers in England that supply end-users in Great Britain.

Transport

In 2010, the United Kingdom met 14.1 TWh of energy demand in the transport sector from renewables, equivalent to 3.6% of total demand, up from 0.2% in 2005. The NREAP targets a renewables contribution to road transport fuels of 10% by 2020, in line with the EU target. Within the UK overall target, bioethanol consumption is to amount to 1 743 ktoe by 2020, of which 83% is expected to be imported. Biodiesel consumption is targeted to rise to 2 462 ktoe, of which 91% is expected to be imported. Electric vehicles are expected to use 267 ktoe.

Before April 2010, a 20 pence per litre duty exemption existed to support biofuel use. This has been superseded by the renewable transport fuel obligation (RTFO), introduced by the Renewable Fuels Agency within the Department of Transport. The RTFO obliges all suppliers of transport fuel volumes of more than 450 000 litres per year to source an increasing percentage of their total supply by volume from renewable energy sources.

Owners of renewable fuels are generally awarded one renewable transport fuel certificate (RTFC) per litre of biofuel, or kilogram of biomethane, at the duty point.[13] The duty point occurs in three cases: when fuel is produced in the United Kingdom and supplied across the duty point into the domestic market; when fuel is imported into the United Kingdom and supplied to the domestic market; and when fuel is purchased in a UK "tax warehouse" and supplied to the domestic market.

All suppliers of biofuels may take part in the scheme, and can claim RTFCs when they cross a duty point, enabling all suppliers and producers of biofuels to trade with suppliers who are below their quota obligation.

---

13. The point when a fuel becomes chargeable for duty. As of December 2011, additional certificates were awarded for the supply of highly sustainable (non-food) biofuel derived from wastes, residues, non-food cellulosic material and ligno-cellulosic material.

In 2011/12, the obligation amounted to 4.1% of road transport fuel by volume. It will increase to 5.3% in 2013/14. Failure to comply incurs a penalty in the form of a buy-out price, which currently is GBP 0.3 per litre. As in the Renewables Obligation, funds under the buy-out mechanism are distributed among renewable fuel suppliers on a pro rata basis according to the number of RTFCs they present to the administrator.

In its 2011 spending review, the government confirmed some GBP 400 million of support for "ultra low-emission vehicles" over the course of the present Parliament. Within this basket is the Plug-In Car Grant Scheme, launched in January 2011, which provides a 25% grant to buyers of hydrogen-fuelled, hybrid and electric vehicles, up to a ceiling of GBP 5 000.

FINANCING AND PROJECT DEVELOPMENT

The principal sources of public funding for deployment of renewable energy technologies are the Renewables Obligation in the electricity sector, the feed-in tariff, the Renewable Heat Incentive and the Renewable Transport Fuels Obligation. In addition to these and other schemes discussed, the following schemes are also relevant:

- the Rural Development Programme for England 2007 to 2013 supports small-scale energy projects (not only renewables) and includes the Energy Crops Scheme;

- Carbon Trust grants for the development of advanced biofuels (2009 to 2011);

- a number of other mechanisms operated at the devolved administrative level: Better Woodlands for Wales; Scottish Biomass Heat Support Scheme; Northern Ireland Biomass Processing Challenge Fund; Community and Renewable Energy Scheme; and the Wave and Tidal Energy Research and Development Scheme; and

- the UK NREAP states that the European Investment Bank will provide up to GBP 700 million for onshore wind projects during the three years following its publication, which was in July 2010.

The government has announced the establishment of a Green Investment Bank, pending approval under EU state aid regulation. Considered to be the first of its kind in the world, the bank is intended above all to mobilise private sector funds into renewable energy investments. It is intended to operate at "arm's length" from government, although strategic objectives will be set in consultation with ministers.

It is hoped that the bank will be able to tackle market failures not addressed directly by government policy. Various vehicles are envisaged to achieve this. To attract traditionally more risk-averse investors, the bank will target the provision of "first loss" debt. An up-front refinancing commitment is being considered, which would serve to guarantee an exit for long-term bank finance once construction has been completed, possibly targeting offshore wind projects. Equity or senior debt injections could be considered for offshore wind and waste-to-energy projects. Other mechanisms are also under consideration.

EU state aid approval is anticipated in the second quarter of 2013. In the meantime, the government announced in December 2011 that it would make direct investments in green infrastructure through its UK Green Investments project. A qualified project could have access to GBP 100 million of government funds for investment in fully commercial waste infrastructure projects and for co-investment in offshore wind projects. These are expected to remain the focus of the bank, once inaugurated, up to 2016.

Public sector capitalisation of the bank would initially amount to GBP 3 billion to 2015. Then the bank is expected to be able to borrow to raise further funds, though this is subject to a fall in public sector net debt as a percentage of GDP and to the granting of further approval under EU state aid rules.

CRITIQUE

There is a great deal of activity in the United Kingdom to accelerate the deployment of renewable energy technologies. Much of it relates to the review of payment mechanisms, both to increase their effectiveness and to reduce windfall effects. At the same time, reform of the electricity market has been undertaken, in which renewable energy technologies are targeted to play an increasingly important role.

Through the introduction of the Renewables Obligation (RO) and measures to address barriers to increased deployment, renewable electricity has become well established in the power sector, quadrupling its share in total electricity generation from 1.8% in 2002 to 7.2% in 2010. However, this falls well short of the targeted 10% of electricity by 2010. While growth rates for renewable electricity capacity in 2010 were higher than those in 2009, a combination of the lowest average wind speeds this century and the lowest rainfall since 2003 impacted on the load factors for wind- and hydropower – with 2011 seeing much higher load factors. IEA analysis suggests that in the case of onshore wind deployment, the shortfall may in fact be due in part to non-economic barriers, such as planning and public acceptance constraints.[14] Furthermore, payments received by projects that have come online in the period have been relatively high and yet overall deployment relatively low, when compared to a number of countries where mainly feed-in tariff schemes are in place.

With the introduction of technology banding in 2009, the RO has been an effective stimulus to the United Kingdom's potentially large offshore wind industry. Indeed the United Kingdom is now the global leader in offshore wind with nearly 2 GW of installed capacity in early 2012, while additional projects in the pipeline amount to over 6 GW.

Nevertheless, deployment of renewables will need to increase sharply over the next decade to meet the indicative level of more than 30% of electricity by 2020. To mobilise greater investment, the government plans to move to a contract-for-difference feed-in tariff model, which may improve the revenue certainty of renewable generation projects. One key challenge will be to set the "strike price" (the contracted MWh price received by the generator) at a level that reflects the real generation costs plus the required return, not least of all because this will need to evolve to encourage future cost reductions.

Care needs to be taken not to startle investors when changing the form of public support to renewable energy technologies. The use of leading indicators (for example the monitoring of consented, rather than already commissioned, projects) would indicate the extent to which this is occurring.

Unexpected rapid reduction in the price of solar PV modules led to overheating in the UK's PV market in 2010-2011, as in other countries. Consequently, the government has reduced the feed-in tariff payable to new PV projects over 50 kW and is expected to

14. *Deploying Renewables 2011 – Best and Future Policy Practice*. IEA/OECD Paris, 2011.

introduce further cuts for smaller projects in late 2011. Although this has caused concern in the PV industry, there can be no doubt that tariffs must evolve to reflect reductions in technology costs.

Offshore wind energy costs have been inflated beyond the level that reflects simple technology cost, by constraints in the supply chain (and to some degree by a weakened currency). Industrial policy should support government ambitions for the technology (increased from 13 GW by 2020 to 18 GW in the July 2011 Renewable Energy Roadmap) by focusing on measures to strengthen the supply chain. Recently announced financing for new and upgraded port facilities should be complemented by a push to develop turbine testing and manufacturing facilities in the United Kingdom. Present uncertainties with regard to the planning framework and the functioning of the future Major Infrastructure Planning Unit will also need to be resolved.

The "connect and manage" transmission access regime adopted in 2009 has materially benefited the wind power project pipeline, to the extent that access to the grid is no longer considered a serious obstacle to 2020 deployment targets. The "bootstraps" under consideration to accommodate increasing flows of electricity between Scotland and England may provide a practical solution to difficulties relating to public acceptance of new transmission system infrastructure. It is to be hoped that in their development, full consideration would be given to further transmission development offshore to connect new generation plants. In this sense, these bootstraps may represent the germ of an offshore grid.

The United Kingdom is to be commended for its efforts to decarbonise the heat sector, which has been largely overlooked in IEA countries historically. Now introduced, its innovative Renewable Heat Incentive will provide a valuable test case: the 12% renewable heat target could represent a major nationwide shift in consumer behaviour. This is a considerable challenge, and one that will be compounded with limited data availability on energy use in the heating sector, and the continuing struggle to encourage improved insulation in UK homes.

The United Kingdom's 10% target for renewable energy use in the transport sector represents a major challenge. Up to 2030 the focus appears to be on biofuels, as a transition in the longer term to electrification (of the car sector). But there is concern that while biofuels sustainability criteria have been successful in increasing the overall carbon savings of indigenously produced biofuels, they may also inadvertently be giving unfair advantage to cheaper imports that are not subject to the same criteria, undermining the overall sustainability of biofuels use. Additionally, concerns remain as to the extent to which domestic biofuels production will shift land use away from other strategic uses, such as food production.

The government has not yet revealed how it intends to support renewables deployment for transport in the period 2014 to 2020, nor where the focus will lie among use of waste, advanced biofuels, hydrogen-fuelled and electric vehicles. It is to be hoped that after the Department for Transport has consulted on the alternatives in 2012, clear legislation will follow quickly.

RECOMMENDATIONS

The government of the United Kingdom should:

☐ *In the context of ongoing electricity market reform, improve the effectiveness of financial support for renewables, maintain investor confidence during the transition to new mechanisms and accelerate deployment to achieve the 2020 target.*

☐ *Rapidly conclude on the renewables in transport pathway for 2014 to 2020.*

☐ *Carefully monitor the Renewable Heat Incentive, including the sufficiency of bioenergy resources and elasticity in consumer behaviour.*

☐ *Address non-financial barriers to the deployment of renewables:*

   o *Green Investment Bank funding should be made available as soon as EU state aid approval has been received.*
   o *Supply chains should be reinforced, particularly in the offshore wind sector.*
   o *Local support for new infrastructure should be encouraged; uncertainty related to institutional change should be minimised.*

9. NUCLEAR ENERGY

Key data (2010)

Number of plants in operation: 10 nuclear power stations

Installed capacity: 10.9 GW

Electricity generation: 62 TWh (16% of total generation)

OVERVIEW

The United Kingdom considers nuclear energy, together with renewable resources and carbon capture and storage (CCS), as key elements to reduce carbon dioxide (CO_2) emissions by 80% by 2050. This target essentially implies the decarbonisation of the power sector by 2030. It is government policy that new nuclear power should be able to contribute as much as possible to the country's need for new capacity.[15]

This policy follows on from the previous government's 2008 White Paper *Meeting the Energy Challenge.* This set out the clear division of responsibilities between the public and the private sectors. The government is responsible for the necessary institutional and market reforms and defining policies for nuclear waste disposal and decommissioning. In October 2010, the Secretary of State for Energy and Climate Change set out that there will be no public subsidy for new nuclear power plants.[16] Financing has to be by the private sector, including the full costs of decommissioning and their full share of waste management costs.

The United Kingdom has thus become a widely watched laboratory for the development of nuclear power in a market economy. This development is to take place without public subsidies, but with the underpinning of a stable regulatory framework and within a reformed electricity market, which it is planned will include a carbon price floor and the introduction of new long-term contracts (contracts for difference feed-in tariffs) to provide stable financial incentives to invest in all forms of low-carbon electricity generation (see Chapter 10).

In 2010, nuclear energy produced 62 TWh, 16% of the United Kingdom's electricity supply, slightly below the IEA average of 22%. Currently, ten nuclear power stations with a combined capacity of 11 gigawatts (GW) are operating in the country. The largest nuclear operator is EDF Energy, a wholly owned subsidiary of Electricité de France (EDF), which purchased British Energy Group plc in January 2009. It runs eight nuclear power stations, seven of which are advanced gas-cooled reactors (AGRs) and the remaining one

---

15. http://www.decc.gov.uk/assets/decc/11/meeting-energy-demand/consents-planning/nps2011/1938-overarching-nps-for-energy-en1.pdf

16. http://www.decc.gov.uk/en/content/cms/news/en_statement/en_statement.aspx

is a pressurised water reactor (PWR) at Sizewell B. Two plants operated by Magnox Ltd. run Magnox gas-cooled reactors. The Nuclear Decommissioning Authority (NDA) owns several closed Magnox stations.

The UK reactor fleet is comparatively old. Up to 7.4 GW of existing nuclear capacity will close by 2019. All but one of the current fleet will have closed by 2023 as the gas-cooled reactors reach the end of their 40-year life. The exception is the 1 200 MW PWR at Sizewell B whose scheduled lifetime is to 2035. Energy companies have at present announced ambitions to construct up to 16 GW of new nuclear capacity, with the first station coming on stream from 2019, at an estimated cost of about GBP 50 billion. Stations have been proposed in England and Wales only. The devolved Scottish government does not support nuclear new build.

INSTITUTIONS

In recent years, the government has taken a number of important steps to create a transparent and coherent regulatory framework to enable the construction of new nuclear capacity and to eliminate uncertainties pertaining to waste disposal and decommissioning. The government has created the **Nuclear Decommissioning Authority** to manage legacy sites, established a process to identify a suitable site for the geological disposal of high-level radioactive wastes, issued a national nuclear policy statement and strengthened the regulatory authority. These efforts are widely recognised.

The interim **Office for Nuclear Regulation** (ONR) was launched in April 2011 as an agency within the **Health and Safety Executive** (HSE) until relevant legislation allowing it to function as a statutory corporation has been enacted. The establishment of the statutory ONR is a joint policy initiative between the Department of Energy and Climate Change (DECC) and the Department for Work and Pensions. ONR brings together the safety and security functions of HSE's Nuclear Directorate, incorporating the Nuclear Installations Inspectorate, Office of Civil Nuclear Security and the UK Safeguards Office. Since October 2011 the ONR has also had responsibility for the regulation of transport of radioactive materials by road, rail and inland waterways, which were previously dealt with by the Department for Transport's Radioactive Materials Transport Division (now part of the ONR). The **Chief Inspector of Nuclear Installations**, who also heads the ONR, has the power to issue, add conditions to and revoke nuclear site licences.

RADIOACTIVE SUBSTANCES

Regulatory oversight for radiological protection rests with the Environment Agency (in England and Wales), the Scottish Environmental Protection Agency (in Scotland) and the Northern Ireland Environment Agency (in Northern Ireland), while medical radioisotopes continue to be dealt with by the HSE. The Environment Agencies oversee the implementation of the Environmental Permitting Regulations of 2010, which replace the Radioactive Substances Act of 1993 (RSA 93) in England and Wales (RSA 93 remains in force in Scotland and Northern Ireland). The Environment Agencies oversee radioactive waste disposal at the United Kingdom's 32 nuclear sites, including site permits. It also regulates the storage and use of radioactive substances for non-nuclear users of radioactive materials such as hospitals and universities, while the ONR oversees the storage and use of radioactive substances at licensed nuclear sites. ONR and the Environment Agencies co-operate in fulfilling their respective missions.

NUCLEAR POWER PLANT CONSTRUCTION

The *Fifth National Report on Compliance with the Convention on Nuclear Safety Obligations,* published in 2010, details the administrative approach to regulating new nuclear power plants, including the generic design assessment. Under the previous government, the Planning Act of 2008 initiated major planning reform in England and Wales and gave a key role for deciding on nationally significant infrastructure, including nuclear power plants, to the Infrastructure Planning Commission (IPC). The new government, however, announced that the IPC will become the Major Infrastructure Planning Unit (MIPU) within the Planning Inspectorate, an agency of the Department for Communities and Local Government. MIPU will consider applications and make recommendations – but decisions will be taken by ministers. In July 2011, the government issued the Energy National Policy Statements, including the Nuclear National Policy Statement. These provide planning guidance that the IPC, and subsequently MIPU, will use in considering applications for new nuclear power plants. The Nuclear National Policy Statement includes the eight sites the government thinks are potentially suitable for deployment by 2025.

RADIOACTIVE WASTE MANAGEMENT AND DECOMMISSIONING

The NDA has responsibility for radioactive waste management and decommissioning, and for nuclear legacy sites. It is a non-departmental public body created in 2005 that employs about 200 people. NDA owns former nuclear sites and the associated civil nuclear liabilities and assets of the public sector, including all the former sites and reactors of British Nuclear Fuels Limited (BNFL) and the UK Atomic Energy Authority (UKAEA). Its responsibilities include decommissioning and clean-up of these installations and sites, as well as the implementation of the UK nuclear waste policy.

Since 1959, most low-level waste (LLW) has been sent to the Low Level Waste Repository near Drigg in west Cumbria (north-west England). NDA's decommissioning programme is likely to generate large additional amounts of LLW. NDA published the UK *Strategy for the Management of Solid LLW from the Nuclear Industry* in 2010. It sets out a number of techniques and technologies to reduce the volumes of LLW requiring disposal, such as sorting and segregation, compaction or thermal treatment, and recycling of metals and soil.

UK policy related to higher activity waste is contained in the 2008 White Paper *Managing Radioactive Waste Safely*. It sets out a process for implementing geological disposal as the preferred method for the long-term management of higher activity waste, coupled with safe and secure interim storage. Concomitantly, communities were invited to express interest in talking to government about the possibility of hosting a geological disposal facility (GDF). The current indicative timetable anticipates a site for a GDF being determined by around 2025 and disposal of intermediate-level waste beginning around 2040 (see Figure 33). Responsibility for planning and implementing geological disposal lies with the NDA. Governance is provided through the Geological Disposal Implementation Board (GDIB), which is chaired by the DECC Minister of State and meets every six months.

Figure 33. **Indicative timeline for implementing geological nuclear waste disposal site**

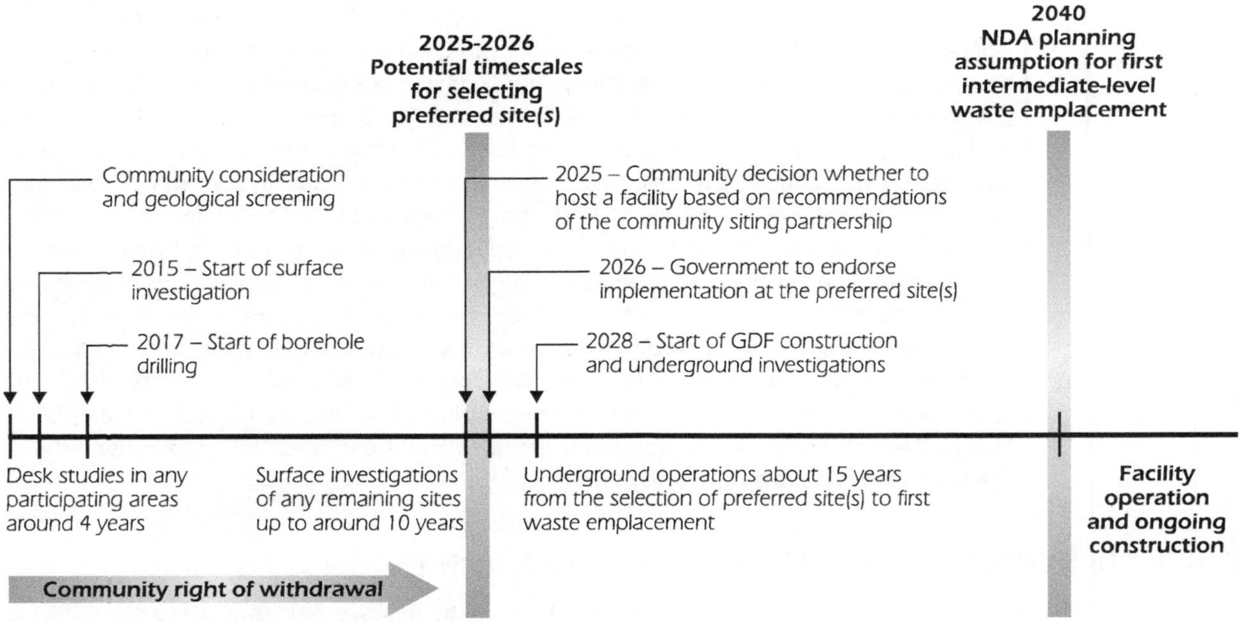

Source: The Nuclear Decommissioning Authority.

Decommissioning the Sellafield site, which includes the THORP reprocessing plant, a technically demanding challenge whose completion could take up to 25 years, is a priority for the NDA. The NDA works by contracting out site operation to management companies. It is currently working on an annual budget of between GBP 2 and 3 billion (see Box 4), but funding remains an issue as resources limit the speed of progress, for instance in the case of the dismantling of the Magnox reactors. Funding for the decommissioning of the seven advanced gas-cooled reactors and EDF's one pressurised-water reactor (that once belonged to British Energy) is assured through the Nuclear Liabilities Fund, formerly the Nuclear Generation Decommissioning Fund. Set up in 1996, the fund held assets of GBP 8.6 billion as of March 2011.

Decommissioning liabilities for new nuclear power plants rest with the plant owner. The 2008 Energy Act requires operators to have a Funded Decommissioning Programme (FDP) approved by the DECC Secretary of State before construction of a new nuclear power station can begin. In 2009, the government created an independent advisory body, the Nuclear Liabilities Financing Assurance Board (NLFAB), to advise the government whether the financial arrangements for decommissioning, waste management and disposal contained in the FDPs submitted by operators of new nuclear power stations are sufficiently robust. Guidelines for the approval of FDPs under the 2008 Energy Act were published in December 2011. They require operators to be fully liable for the cost of decommissioning and to constitute funds with corresponding "target values" for assets, including contingencies for risk and uncertainty. The majority of a fund's administrators will have to be independent of both the operator and the government. The latter, by way of the Secretary of State for Energy and Climate Change, will nevertheless verify that appropriate arrangements are in place. Operating under a nuclear site licence without a government-approved FDP is considered an offence under the Energy Act.

Box 4. Activities of the Nuclear Decommissioning Authority

The NDA's strategic role in structuring the UK nuclear sector is exemplified by a number of initiatives. For example, it

- awarded a contract to operate the low-level waste repository to UK Nuclear Waste Management Ltd. in 2008;

- awarded a contract to operate the Sellafield site to Nuclear Management Partners Ltd. in 2008;

- established URENCO Chemplants Ltd. as a wholly owned subsidiary of URENCO UK Ltd. in 2007 with responsibility for the construction and operation of the Tails Management Facility to deal with by-products of the uranium enrichment process;

- transferred all NDA Capenhurst assets to URENCO UK Ltd., including the management of the infrastructure associated with a decommissioned gaseous diffusion plant;

- established UKAEA Ltd. in 2008. Its subsidiary holds the licence and discharge authorisation for the Dounreay site. UKAEA Ltd. was acquired by Babcock International Group in 2009;

- prepared a single competition for all Magnox sites plus Harwell and Winfrith for 2014;

- created Magnox Ltd. in 2011 combining the sites of Magnox South and Magnox North to allow for better organisational resilience and economies of scale;

- converted management of the Springfield site into a long-term lease.

NEW NUCLEAR CONSTRUCTION AND ELECTRICITY MARKET REFORM

Nuclear energy together with renewables and carbon capture and storage are central to the United Kingdom's strategy to achieve ambitious greenhouse gas reduction targets and to develop low-carbon technologies. However, the UK reactor fleet is comparatively old and all but one of its existing nuclear power stations will close by 2023. The government has taken forward a series of facilitative actions to encourage nuclear new build, and industry has announced ambitions for construction of up to 16 GW by 2025. The first reactor is scheduled to go online in 2019. New nuclear investments will be part of the total GBP 75 billion estimated for new power generating capacity needed by 2020. Two consortia are currently preparing for the construction of new nuclear power plants, and a third consortium and associated sites is being put up for sale:

- EDF intends to build four European pressurised-water reactors at Hinkley Point and Sizewell with a combined capacity of 6.4 GW.

- NuGen, a joint venture of GDF Suez and Iberdrola, intends to build 3.6 GW of new capacity at Sellafield.

- Horizon Nuclear Power, a joint venture between E.ON and RWE nPower, has plans to develop at least 6GW of new capacity at Wylfa and Oldbury. However, in March 2012 E.ON and RWE announced that they would be withdrawing from new nuclear in the United Kingdom and putting Horizon and its sites up for sale.

Among the three consortia, EDF is moving forward the fastest, having made an application for development consent to the Infrastructure Planning Commission in December 2011.

Much of the future of nuclear energy in the United Kingdom hinges on the precise conditions of the government's announced reform of the electricity and carbon markets to promote low-carbon technologies. The 2011 White Paper *Planning Our Electric Future: a White Paper for Secure, Affordable and Low-Carbon Electricity* spelled out that the key element of the reform would consist of long-term feed-in tariffs (FiTs) with contracts for difference (FiT CfD) which would guarantee low-carbon producers (including nuclear power producers) a fixed "strike price" over the contract (see Chapter 10). Coupled with a gradually rising price floor in the carbon market and a yet-to-be created capacity market, these reforms should make nuclear energy an attractive option for private investors.

The precise arrangements surrounding the contracts for difference are still subject to discussion. These include the level of the strike price, the process for setting it, possibly through a tender or an auction, and the institutional arrangements required to handle multi-billion transfers over many years. From the point of view of the operator, the contract-for-difference part of a FiT CfD is particularly attractive, since it provides financial and legal certainty over long time-frames, especially if coupled with a volume guarantee.[17] Standard feed-in tariffs can be revoked through a routine regulatory or legal change, but legally binding private contracts that were cleared by a counter party independent of the UK Treasury would provide a significantly higher degree of certainty.

For the operator, a FiT CfD is also preferable to a premium FiT (PFiT), which pays the operator a fixed premium over the market price. The PFit stabilises minimum revenue, but not average revenue and leaves a financial downside risk. If wholesale prices rise, a FiT CfD should be able to generate the same risk reduction benefit for the operator at an overall lower financial exposure for the government. CfDs might also have the beneficial side-effect of allowing for increased competition at all levels of the electricity value chain, since they would remove the need for electricity producers to hedge themselves against wholesale price risk through vertical integration all along the value chain, including retail operations. The UK electricity markets are today dominated by the vertically integrated big six utilities, and the wholesale market is small and illiquid, a configuration that has recently come under increasing scrutiny by the public, politicians and regulators alike.

In the 2011 White Paper, the government proposes that contracts for difference would be available for all major low-carbon technologies, nuclear, renewables and CCS. This measure is deemed necessary to overcome the intrinsic disadvantage of low-carbon technologies in a free-market environment, namely a high ratio of fixed costs to variable costs, which makes such technologies vulnerable to the risk of sudden changes in electricity prices. Logically FiT CfDs would only be available for new plants. In the absence of such stabilising measures, natural gas would be the fuel of choice for much of the required new investment, given the price uncertainty in the volatile UK power market. Even a carbon price on its own might not be able to overcome this bias. This in

---

17. The question of whether metered output shall be remunerated at the strike price or whether the CfD should be specified in terms of a firm volume is still being discussed (February 2012). In principle, the former solution seems more appropriate to variable renewable energy sources, whereas the latter seems more appropriate for nuclear energy with largely predictable volumes of production.

return would pose issues for the security of energy supply. Only the combination of the three main measures of the UK electricity market reform – contracts for difference, carbon price floor and capacity market – is deemed to be able to fully internalise the negative externalities of climate change and the security of supply risk.

From the point of view of the government, the CfDs for low-carbon technologies would ideally be technology-neutral. However, a first round of bidding will certainly involve differentiated strike prices offered to nuclear, renewables and CCS. In this line-up, nuclear is considered the most cost-effective low-carbon technology, before onshore wind, whereas offshore wind and CCS are considered more expensive. There is hope that the risk reduction inherent in CfDs would also reduce costs of financing low-carbon technologies across the board and that one day, a single CfD tender will be held for all technologies. However, in the near term, CfDs would be required to spur much needed investment. Owing to the pending closure of existing plants, including coal and nuclear plants, de-rated capacity margins will fall from today's 20% to as low as 5% in some years by the end of the decade.

NUCLEAR RESEARCH

In the United Kingdom, nuclear energy is considered an industrial matter. Therefore, there is no public funding of basic research and development (R&D) for nuclear outside academia. Public spending on applied R&D, which had increased in recent years mainly thanks to research funding through the NDA, is also due to decrease. For applied research, the UK National Nuclear Laboratory (NNL) was created in 2008 by a merger of Nexia Solutions, originally operated by BNFL, with the British Technology Centre. The NNL is financed by industry and concentrates on applied research with direct industrial uses. It employs about 800 people. In addition, the ONR has a research budget of about GBP 35 million, which allows funding of nuclear safety research. The approach to rely on industry funding in most nuclear energy matters extends even to UK membership in some international organisations, such as the OECD Nuclear Energy Agency.

HUMAN CAPITAL

As in other countries with a sizeable nuclear industry, a large share of nuclear engineers is nearing retirement. Their knowledge and experience will be withdrawing from the highly specialised workforce at a time when the UK nuclear sector faces the double challenge of an ambitious target of new nuclear power plant construction and a large nuclear decommissioning programme. The government has tried to anticipate and address the threat of skill shortages through the creation of a number of nuclear engineering programmes at universities, the Nuclear Skills Academy and the National Nuclear Laboratory. Responding to active government encouragement, the universities of Birmingham, Lancaster and Manchester have added degree courses in nuclear engineering in recent years and student numbers are increasing. In the Nuclear Skills Academy, qualified "trainers" transmit the required knowledge for future employees of the nuclear industry, which are certified with the help of a Nuclear Skills Passport. The Nuclear Skills Academy is sponsored by the Nuclear Energy Skills Alliance, which brings together public and private actors to identify risks in the area of nuclear skills and to recommend mitigating actions. The NDA launched its own Skills and Capability Strategy in 2008 with a budget of more than GBP 40 million.

PUBLIC OPINION

Over the years, public opinion in the United Kingdom has been broadly in favour of nuclear power. This positive attitude has held up and even increased in the wake of the Fukushima Dai-ichi nuclear power accident in Japan in March 2011. An independent poll of 2 050 people commissioned by the British Science Association and carried out at the end of August 2011 showed that 41% believe that the benefits of nuclear outweigh the risks, compared with 38% in 2010. On the contrary, the share of those who believe that the risks outweigh the benefits dropped from 36% in 2010 to 28%. Local and regional support around potential sites also holds up well as potential investors such as EDF at Hinkley Point explain at length the advantages of major nuclear investment for businesses, jobs and communities.

In October 2011, the United Kingdom's Chief Inspector of Nuclear Installations and executive head of the Office for Nuclear Regulation released a report on the implications of the Fukushima Dai-ichi accident. The report was prepared at the request of the Secretary of State for Energy and Climate Change to assess the lessons of the accident for the national nuclear safety regime as well as to integrate any relevant findings for the UK nuclear programme. The report found no significant weakness in the level of safety of UK nuclear plants, but highlighted a number of areas for improvement such as flood risks, plant layout and emergency preparedness. The report is unlikely to dent the positive attitude to nuclear power of the UK public.

CRITIQUE

Nuclear energy for electricity generation is a key technology in the government's strategy to enhance energy security and achieve its climate change objectives. This presents significant challenges, particularly in light of the advanced age of the existing nuclear power plant fleet and the fact that a substantial amount of coal-fired power capacity is due to be retired or will have capacity availability curtailed in the coming years. Government policy, set out in the Nuclear National Policy Statement, is that new nuclear power should be able to contribute as much as possible to the United Kingdom's need for new capacity. The previous government's Nuclear White Paper set out a clear division between the public and private sectors. Government is responsible for establishing adequate institutional and market reforms and to define national policies for nuclear waste disposal and decommissioning. New nuclear build is to be financed and operated by the private sector without public subsidies.

It is widely recognised, including by the nuclear industry, that in the last few years the government has undertaken a number of important initiatives to underpin this strategy. It has created appropriate institutional infrastructure and eliminated barriers that may have contributed to uncertainties in the planning and licensing process or due to open questions pertaining to waste disposal and decommissioning. For example, it created the Nuclear Decommissioning Authority to manage legacy sites; it awarded management contracts for nuclear decommissioning, waste management and fuel services for a number of legacy sites; it set out a process for identifying an appropriate geological disposal site for high-level radioactive waste; and it is working to create the nuclear regulator as an independent statutory body responsible for delivering its regulatory functions. The government has also introduced a legislative framework to ensure that operators of new nuclear power stations meet the full cost of decommissioning, waste management and disposal by providing ring-fenced financial security.

The present timetable for selecting the site for the geological disposal of high-level radioactive wastes is by 2025. This does not seem overly ambitious considering the site's crucial role for the public acceptance of nuclear power. The government is therefore encouraged to consider setting an earlier deadline for selecting the site. The IEA urges the government also to further develop the compensation packages for local and regional communities that host nuclear plants or waste disposal sites.

The threat of nuclear skill shortages is being addressed through the creation of several nuclear engineering programmes at universities and specific nuclear academies. However, the government needs to carefully monitor the success of these initiatives relative to the retirement rate of the workforce from industry and research institutions. While the government has had an understandable focus on legacy issues and the commencement of new build, there is a need to provide advice and support in developing long-term policy priorities. This includes nuclear research. Hence, the government should reconsider the management, funding and priority setting for UK nuclear research. It would also benefit from intensifying its engagement in international organisations, such as the International Atomic Energy Agency and the OECD Nuclear Energy Agency for further co-ordinated research and regulatory activities.

The challenge for nuclear energy in the United Kingdom is economic rather than political or social. Much of the future for nuclear energy in the country will hinge on the outcome of the current discussions about the government's announced reform of the electricity and carbon markets to promote low-carbon technologies. A key element of these reforms may consist of long-term contracts for difference that would guarantee nuclear power producers a fixed strike price. Coupled with a gradually rising price floor in the carbon market, this should make nuclear energy an attractive option for private investors. The extent to which a planned capacity mechanism will impact the profitability of nuclear energy will depend on the details, which are currently under discussion.

RECOMMENDATIONS

The government of the United Kingdom should:

☐ *Consider setting an earlier deadline for selecting the geological disposal site for high-level radioactive wastes.*

☐ *Further develop the compensation packages for local and regional communities that host nuclear plants or waste disposal sites; and do this in an equitable and transparent manner.*

☐ *In the light of the need to provide advice and support in developing policy priorities, set a longer-term strategy for the management, funding and priority setting for UK nuclear research.*

☐ *Leverage its engagement in international organisations such as the International Atomic Energy Agency and the OECD Nuclear Energy Agency for further co-ordinated research and regulatory activities.*

10. ELECTRICITY

Key data (2010)

Installed capacity: 93.4 GW

Total electricity generation: 378 TWh

Peak demand: 60.9 GW

Electricity generation mix: natural gas 46%, coal 29%, nuclear 16%, biofuels and waste 4%, wind 3%, oil 1%, hydro 1%

SUPPLY AND DEMAND

SUPPLY

Electricity generation in the United Kingdom was 378 terawatt-hours (TWh) in 2010, about the same level as in 2000 and 4% lower than the historical record of 395 TWh in 2003 and 2005. The government projects a slight decrease in electricity generation over the next decade.

Natural gas dominates the United Kingdom's electricity supply, generating 175 TWh and accounting for 46% of total generation in 2010 (Figure 34), up from about 40% in 2000. Coal accounts for 29% of the fuel mix and generated 109 TWh in 2010. Coal's share in the power mix has declined steadily over the last two decades and this decline is expected to continue, owing to plant closures later this decade. Nuclear accounts for 16% of the electricity mix and generated 62 TWh in 2010. The nuclear share is down from 23% in 2000 and is expected to decrease further by 2020 as power plants are reaching the end of their operating lifetime. Other contributors to electricity generation in 2010 include biofuels and waste (3.5%); wind (2.7%); oil (1.3%) and hydropower (1%). Electricity generation from renewable sources will have to multiply in volume for the United Kingdom to meet its 2020 targets for the share of renewable energy in gross total final consumption of energy (see Chapter 8).

Among the 28 IEA member countries, the United Kingdom ranks seventh in the share of fossil fuels in electricity generation, between Greece and Turkey (Figure 35). The contribution of renewables to UK power supply is low in this group, ranking only slightly better than Poland and the Czech Republic.

While electricity imports have declined over the last decade, the United Kingdom remains a net electricity importer (2.9 TWh in 2009 and 2.7 TWh 2010). Imports come mainly from France, while exports go to Ireland. Since April 2011, a cross-border connection with the Netherlands is in operation.

Figure 34. **Electricity generation by source, 1973 to 2020**

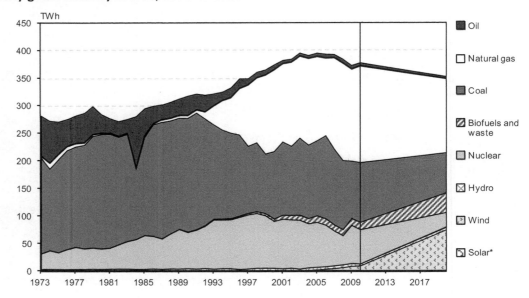

* Negligible.

Sources: *Energy Balances of OECD Countries*, IEA/OECD Paris, 2011 and country submission.

Figure 35. **Breakdown of electricity generation by source in IEA countries, 2010***

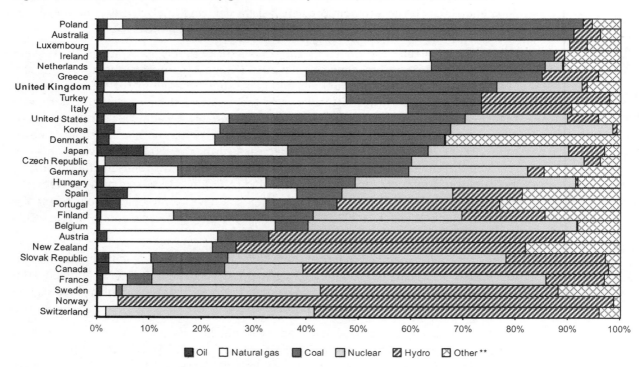

* Estimates.

** *Other* includes geothermal, solar, wind and ambient heat production.

Source: *Energy Balances of OECD Countries*, IEA/OECD Paris, 2011.

GENERATING CAPACITY

At the end of 2010, the United Kingdom's net maximum generating capacity was 93.4 gigawatts (GW), an increase of 5.9 GW from 2009, according to IEA data.[18] This total capacity includes 34 GW of combined-cycle gas-turbine plants (CCGTs), 24 GW of coal-fired capacity and 11 GW of nuclear. The rest is dual-fired, oil-fired and renewable capacity. Installed wind capacity was 5.4 GW in 2010, ranking sixth among IEA countries, with similar levels in France at 5.7 GW and Italy at 5.8 GW. Wind power capacity is much higher in the leading IEA countries with 27.2 GW in Germany and 20.8 GW in Spain.

By 2020, around a fifth of the United Kingdom's electricity generating capacity is expected to be closed. According to the November 2011 Statutory Security of Supply Report by DECC and Ofgem, the EU Large Combustion Plant Directive will lead to closure of around 12 GW of coal- and oil-fired capacity, considered too polluting by modern standards, before 2016. The EU Industrial Emissions Directive could also lead to further closures by 2023 (see Chapter 6 for a detailed description of the directives' requirements). In addition, up to 7.1 GW of nuclear capacity is reaching the end of its operational life and will have closed by 2020. Some 19.1 GW could therefore close by 2020, with further closures by 2023.

On the other hand, around 8.3 GW of new capacity that will connect to the transmission system was already being built in November 2011; 4.3 GW of this is gas-fired and 3.6 GW is renewable generation capacity. A further 13.2 GW has planning permission, of which 8.7 GW is gas-fired and 3.7 GW is renewable capacity. Replacement of nuclear capacity may also be constructed by around 2025, following the electricity market reforms.

In any case, DECC expects the de-rated capacity margin[19] to fall from around 17% today to some 5% around the middle of the next decade, increasing the likelihood of costly blackouts. Under some scenarios, this could happen much sooner. This level is considered too low and the government has decided to introduce a capacity mechanism as part of the electricity market reform (see below).

DEMAND

Electricity demand is highest in the residential sector and accounts for 36% of total electricity consumption (Figure 36). This ranks second among IEA countries and is only slightly lower than France where the household sector demand is 38% of the total. The industry sector accounts for 32% of electricity demand, which is among the lowest shares in IEA countries. The commercial and services sector (*Other*) accounted for 29% in 2010, the remainder being consumed in the transport (1%) and agriculture and fishing sectors (1%).

The government forecasts that the industrial sector will have a larger share of electricity demand in 2020. The outlook is for a lower share in the residential sector, dropping to 27% by 2020, a lower share than at anytime in recent decades.

---

18. IEA capacity figures are the sum of all individual plants' maximum capacities available to run continuously throughout a prolonged period of operation in a day. *i.e.* non-derated. The de-rated figures for 2010 are 90.2 GW and 5.4 GW.

19. The capacity margin adjusted to take account of the probable technical availability of plant, specific to each type of generation technology.

Per-capita electricity consumption in the United Kingdom was around 5 350 kilowatt-hour (kWh) in 2010. This is much lower than the IEA average of 8 200 kWh per person, reflecting a lower electricity intensity in industry and heating in the United Kingdom.

Figure 36. **Electricity consumption by sector, 1973 to 2020**

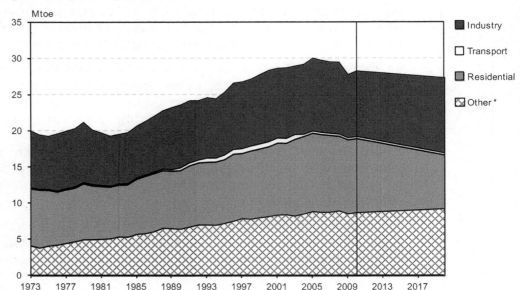

* *Other* includes commercial, public service, agricultural, fishing and other non-specified sectors.

Sources: *Energy Balances of OECD Countries*, IEA/OECD Paris, 2011 and country submission.

According to DECC's Digest of United Kingdom Energy Statistics, the maximum demand in the United Kingdom during the winter of 2010/11 occurred on 7 December 2010. At 60 893 MW, this was 1.1% higher than the previous winter's maximum on 7 January 2010. In 2010/11, the maximum load in Great Britain occurred on 7 December 2010 at the half-hour period ending 17:30 (59 130 MW). However, in Northern Ireland the maximum load occurred on 22 December 2010 at the period ending 18:00 (1 777 MW), which was 3.3% above that of the previous winter. In Great Britain the highest ever load met was 60,118 MW on 10 December 2002. Maximum demand in 2010/11 was 73% of the UK capacity of major power producers as measured at the end of December 2010.

MARKET DESIGN AND STRUCTURE

REGULATION

The legal base for the UK electricity sector is provided in several pieces of legislation, namely the Electricity Act 1989 (as amended), the Utilities Act 2000 and Energy Acts 2004, 2008, 2010 and 2011. As a member state of the European Union, the United Kingdom has to transpose the EU directives on the electricity sector into national law, while EU regulations apply directly.

Generation and supply are unbundled from transmission and distribution. Each function is also licensed separately by the Office of Gas and Electricity Markets (Ofgem), the regulator. The licensees are also required to become parties to the industry codes that detail the rules and terms that underpin the functioning of the electricity system and the electricity market.

Ofgem is the regulator for electricity and natural gas in Great Britain. Under statute, its principal duty is to protect the interests of consumers by promoting competition wherever appropriate. It is also responsible for effective regulation of the monopoly companies which control the gas and electricity networks. It does this by setting price controls for these companies. More generally, businesses are required to be licensed in order to participate in GB energy markets and Ofgem administers the licensing system, imposing a number of standard and special licence conditions in line with its objectives. Ofgem's regulation is funded through licence revenues which it collects directly from licence holders. Ofgem is responsible for the appointments of its staff, including the Chief Executive and other senior staff.

MARKET DESIGN OVERVIEW

The electricity market in the United Kingdom is divided into two parts geographically. Great Britain has a single electricity market, while Northern Ireland forms an all-island electricity market with the Republic of Ireland. The electricity supply industry in Northern Ireland has been in private ownership since 1993 with Northern Ireland Electricity plc (NIE) responsible for power procurement, transmission, distribution and supply in the province. Generation is provided by three private companies which own the four major power stations. In December 2001, the link between Northern Ireland's grid and that of Scotland was inaugurated. A link between the Northern Ireland grid and that of the Irish Republic was re-established in 1996, along which electricity is both imported and exported. However, on 1 November 2007 the two grids were fully integrated and a joint body SEMO (Single Electricity Market Operator) was set up by SONI (System Operator for Northern Ireland) and Eirgrid from the Republic of Ireland to oversee the new single market. The rest of this chapter will focus on the electricity market in Great Britain.

The GB electricity market is divided into:

- the wholesale market where generators, suppliers and large customers buy and sell electricity;

- transmission and distribution networks at national and regional levels; and

- the retail market, where energy suppliers sell to domestic and business customers.

WHOLESALE MARKET

The current market has developed following liberalisation in the 1990s. The intention was to create a competitive electricity system where prices are determined without administrative prices or other regulatory interventions and where those real-time unfettered movements in price, and the freedom of market participants' actions (including contracting and hedging), would be the main drivers of investment behaviour.

The Energy Act 2004 introduced a single wholesale market system for Great Britain, under the British Electricity Trading and Transmission Arrangements (BETTA). BETTA was launched in April 2005. It replaced the New Electricity Trading Arrangements (NETA) in England and Wales and the separate trading arrangements which operated in Scotland. NETA, in turn, had replaced the previous pool arrangement in 2001.

BETTA is designed to provide:

- a common set of trading rules allowing electricity to be traded freely across Great Britain;
- rules for access to, and charging for, the transmission network; and
- a GB-wide system operator (SO) independent of generation and supply interests.

The wholesale market is designed to be much like a typical commodity market. Generators sell electricity to suppliers through bilateral contracts, over-the-counter (OTC) trades and spot markets. In 2010, around 91% of all power traded in Great Britain was OTC-traded and around 9% was exchange-traded. There are now three exchange providers in the British electricity market: the APX Group, Nasdaq OMX N2EX and the Intercontinental Exchange (ICE).

In 2010, the largest three companies generated nearly half of electricity consumed in Great Britain and seven companies had market shares exceeding 5% (see Figure 37). The major energy suppliers that dominate retail supply (see below under Retail Market) accounted for around 68% of generation in 2010.

In the wholesale market, electricity is traded in 30-minute blocks (called settlement periods). This continues until an hour before the start of a settlement period (a point called gate closure). After gate closure, the responsibility for ensuring that supply equals demand on a second-by-second basis is held by a central body (National Grid Electricity Transmission, NGET, the system operator). NGET assesses the characteristics of the system and takes balancing actions, mostly using the balancing mechanism, to correct any imbalance.

Figure 37. Breakdown of electricity generation by company, 2010

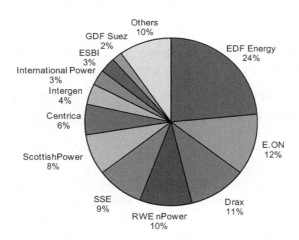

Source: Ofgem.

As in the gas market, imbalance penalties (cash-out prices) are used to provide market participants with strong commercial incentives to balance their contractual and physical positions, either by contracting for supply ahead of time or by maintaining the reliability of their generating plant.

As part of the terms for their connection to the system, generators are required to provide mandatory contracted balancing services according to the terms set out in the Grid Code. The mandatory services cover basic levels of reactive power and frequency response. NGET also contracts with generators and large suppliers to hold a "reserve" to keep the system in balance. These commercial services are either directly negotiated between NGET and the service provider or procured via a tender process.

RETAIL MARKET

The GB retail electricity supply market opened to competition in the late 1990s and all price controls were removed by April 2002. Currently, the retail electricity supply is dominated by six large vertically integrated major energy suppliers which evolved from the fifteen former incumbent electricity and gas suppliers over the 1998-2003 period. These are:

- **Centrica plc:** owns British Gas Trading, which operates three retail brands (British Gas in England, Nwy Prydain in Wales and Scottish Gas in Scotland);

- **E.ON UK:** a wholly-owned subsidiary of the German energy group, which operates under the E.ON brand;

- **EDF Energy:** a wholly-owned subsidiary of the French energy group – it operates under the EDF Energy brand;

- **RWE nPower:** part of the German energy group, RWE Group. The supply business operates under the nPower brand;

- **Scottish and Southern Energy (SSE):** maintains and promotes separate and distinct energy retail brands in England, Scotland and Wales; and

- **ScottishPower:** a wholly-owned subsidiary of the Spanish energy group Iberdrola and operates under the ScottishPower brand.

At the end of 2010, twelve suppliers were active in the residential electricity market. However, more than 99% of the 27.4 million residential electricity customers were supplied by the six largest suppliers (see Figure 38). They are successors to regional monopolies and still retain a strong position in their respective regions.

Figure 38. **Breakdown of the number of residential electricity customers by company, December 2010**

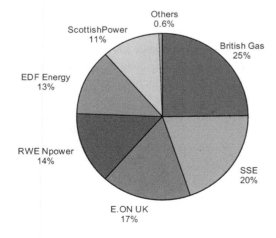

Source: Ofgem.

At the end of 2010, 22 electricity suppliers were active in the non-residential market. The current major energy suppliers together supply 91% to 97% of each market segment (small, medium-sized and large customers). A group of new entrants supplies the rest.

Since May 1999, all of the domestic electricity market in Great Britain has been open to competition. By December 2010, 15.5 million electricity consumers (59%) were no longer with their home supplier. From 2006 to 2010, every year on average more than 18% of household customers switched their supplier.

VERTICAL INTEGRATION AND MARKET LIQUIDITY

Since the late 1990s, vertical reintegration between generating, electricity distribution and/or electricity supply businesses has increased significantly in the British electricity market. The major energy suppliers in the domestic market are vertically integrated, *i.e.* they are part of corporate groups that are active in both the wholesale and retail markets.

Vertically integrated companies do not need to have access to the wholesale market to the same extent as independent suppliers and generators do. In the United Kingdom, the latter have expressed concerns that they find it difficult to manage risk with the wholesale products currently available. This could have a negative impact on the outcomes for consumers in the supply market, especially if it means that there is no viable threat to existing suppliers.

In its 2008 Retail Market Probe and the subsequent 2011 Retail Market Review, Ofgem has assessed the state of competition, consumer experiences of the market and energy market liquidity, including the role of vertical integration. Ofgem found in March 2011 that competition was being stifled by a combination of tariff complexity, poor supplier behaviour and lack of transparency.

As part of the liquidity probe, Ofgem concluded in 2010 that the proportion of exchange trading of total electricity consumption in 2008 and 2009 was significantly lower in Great Britain than in other European market areas (Germany, France, the Netherlands, Nordpool). Liquidity is particularly low in the forward market, *i.e.* for electricity to be delivered in the month ahead and after.

In March 2011, Ofgem proposed two interventions to increase wholesale market liquidity. The proposals were *i)* a mandatory auction in the forward market of up to 20% of generated output from large vertically integrated players, and *II)* mandatory market-making arrangements. Both were intended to provide the liquidity that market participants, in particular independent market players, require to compete effectively, and to encourage competition between vertically integrated players. Ofgem was due to publish more detailed proposals and an impact assessment by the end of 2011.

ELECTRICITY MARKET REFORM

The government is currently detailing plans for a major reform of the electricity market. Following extensive consultations and previous analysis by Ofgem, the government has laid out its proposals for electricity market reform in the July 2011 White Paper (*Planning our Electric Future: a White Paper for secure, affordable and low-carbon electricity*) and the December 2011 technical update to it. This section is largely based on those two documents.

The government has decided that reform is necessary, because:

- Plant closures will threaten security of electricity supply. Over the next decade, the United Kingdom is expected to lose around a fifth (around 19 GW) of its existing generating capacity as old or more polluting plants close (see above under Generating Capacity). This will reduce capacity margins and increase the likelihood of costly blackouts. The future electricity system will also contain more intermittent generation (such as wind) and inflexible generation (such as nuclear). This structure may threaten continuity of supply if there is insufficient investment in generating capacity to meet peak demand periods and/or to replace wind generation when the wind is not blowing.

- Carbon emissions must be reduced. The United Kingdom aims to cut its greenhouse gas emissions by 80% from 1990 to 2050. For this to happen, power sector emissions need to be largely decarbonised by the 2030s. Without reform, the electricity sector would have an emissions intensity in 2030 of over three times the level advised by the Climate Change Committee. As an EU member state, the United Kingdom also must increase the share of renewable energy in gross total final consumption to 15% by 2020. Electricity will be the largest contributor to meeting this target.

- Demand for electricity is likely to rise in the long term, to 2050. Despite the improvements in energy efficiency which will be generated through the introduction of the Green Deal and the roll-out of smart meters (see Chapter 4), overall demand for electricity may double by 2050, because of the electrification of the transport, heat and other carbon-intensive sectors.

- Electricity prices are expected to rise. Increases in wholesale costs, the carbon price and environmental policies are likely to lead to higher bills in the future, even without factoring in the necessary investment in new generation and transmission infrastructure. Ofgem has estimated that around GBP 110 billion of new investment is needed in the period to 2020 – over twice the rate of the last decade.

The electricity market reform comprises the following four new interlocking policy instruments that would give existing players and new entrants in the energy sector the certainty they need to raise the level of investment. They need:

- **A carbon price floor** (CPF) to provide a transparent and predictable carbon price for the medium and long term, something the EU-ETS cannot currently provide. The CPF will gradually increase the wholesale electricity price and should increase investment in low-carbon generation. The CPF will be introduced by removing from the Climate Change Levy (CCL) the current exemption for supplies of fossil fuels which are used to generate electricity in the United Kingdom. The CPF as announced in the Budget 2011 begins at around GBP 15.70 per tCO_2 in 2013 and follows a straight line to GBP 30 per tCO_2 in 2020, rising to GBP 70 per tCO_2 in 2030 (real 2009 prices).

- **A "contract for difference" feed-in tariff** (FiT CfD) which is a long-term contract for stabilising revenue and reducing risks to support investment in all forms of low-carbon electricity generation. If the wholesale electricity price is below the price agreed in the contract (strike price), the generator will receive a top-up payment to make up the difference. If the wholesale price is above the contract price, the generator pays the surplus back.

To reflect the different commercial and operational behaviour among different classes of generation, the government will tailor the design of the FiT CfD for different generation types. The ability to avoid excessive support is a key advantage of the technology-specific FiT CfD compared to a technology-neutral one.

The FiT CfD will provide low-carbon electricity generators with a guaranteed price throughout the period of the long-term contract. It will complement the carbon price floor. As the price of carbon increases and gradually raises the electricity price, the support needed for low-carbon generators through the FiT CfD is reduced.

- **A capacity mechanism** to ensure sufficient reliable and diverse generating capacity to meet demand as the amount of intermittent and inflexible low carbon generation increases. The capacity mechanism will be implemented as a Capacity Market. This will involve contracting the level of diverse capacity required to meet peak demand through a central auction. The Capacity Market would include both generation and non-generation forms of capacity such as demand-side response and storage.

- **An emissions performance standard** (EPS) to limit how much carbon power stations can emit. The EPS will reinforce the existing requirement that no new coal-fired generation is built without carbon capture and storage. It will initially be set at a level equivalent to 450 g CO_2 per kWh (at baseload) for all new fossil fuel plants, except CCS demonstration plants. The EPS will not be retrospective, but it will be subject to regular reviews.

The government has decided to designate the system operator as the body to deliver the Capacity Market and contractual terms for low-carbon generation through the FiT CfD. The government will retain overall accountability, set the policy objectives and take decisions on the key rules and parameters of the mechanisms.

The electricity market reform will be complemented by Ofgem's review into the liquidity of the wholesale electricity market. The FiT CfD requires a robust reference price which reflects market fundamentals and cannot be manipulated. Strong liquidity in the electricity wholesale market is crucial for the FiT CfD to function effectively. The capacity mechanism, too, will benefit from a transparent wholesale market price.

The government will also develop its electricity system policy, looking at the future system and focusing on challenges around balancing and system flexibility. This will include clarifying the role of demand-side response, storage and interconnection, and the development of a smarter grid. Finally, the government is also defining measures to encourage early project development and avoid a prolonged investment hiatus while the details of the reform are pending.

The government expects electricity prices to rise relative to today with or without reform, because of potential increases in the wholesale price of gas, the carbon price and network costs and other policies. However, it expects the implementation of the electricity market reform to reduce average household consumer bills by 4% from what they would have been without the reforms over the period up to 2030.

Key next steps by summer 2012 will be:

- technical details on FiT CfD and EPS (early 2012);

- an electricity market reform policy update (spring 2012);

- further update on enabling investment decisions for early projects (spring 2012); and

- Electricity System Policy document (summer 2012).

The government intends to have primary legislation for key elements of the electricity market reform package adopted by spring 2013.

TRANSMISSION AND DISTRIBUTION

TRANSMISSION SYSTEM

The National Electricity Transmission System (NETS) is used to transfer bulk electricity from generating power stations to substations near demand. The NETS comprises both onshore and offshore transmission networks. NETS includes around 25 000 km of high-voltage overhead lines (275 kilovolts and above in England and Wales and 132 kilovolts and above in Scotland and offshore). Transmission assets onshore are owned and maintained by regulated regional monopoly transmission owners (TOs). Since the granting of the first offshore transmission licence in March 2011 there are now seven TOs:

- National Grid Electricity Transmission Plc (NGET) owns the transmission system in England and Wales;

- SP Transmission Limited (SPTL) owns the transmission system in southern Scotland;

- Scottish Hydro Electric Transmission Limited (SHETL) owns the transmission system in northern Scotland;

- TCP Robin Rigg OFTO Limited;

- TC Barrow OFTO Limited;

- TC Gunfleet Sands OFTO Limited; and

- Blue Transmission Walney 1 Limited.

NGET is the sole system operator (SO) of NETS. It has responsibility for ensuring that electricity supply and demand stay in balance and the system remains within safe technical and operating limits. NGET is part of National Grid which was listed on the London Stock Exchange in 1995 and has a well-diversified ownership base, with the largest owner (BlackRock) holding just over 5% of total voting rights.

NETWORK ACCESS

Electricity transmission is subject to a licence granted by Ofgem. National Grid, in its role as the national electricity transmission system operator, has a duty under its transmission licence to connect all types of new generator to the transmission system when an application is made for connection. The licence requires National Grid to provide new generators with details of the connection charges to be paid and the date

by which the necessary works will be completed to enable connection. It also means...
timetable within which an application will be process...

In August 2010, the government introduced a new enduring "connect and manage" grid access regime, enabling new generation to apply for an accelerated connection based on the time taken to complete their "enabling works". Previously developers had to wait for wider network reinforcement to be carried out before they could be connected. To date, 73 proposed large generation projects – representing a total capacity of 26 GW – have advanced their expected connection dates under "connect and manage" by an average of six years.

NETWORK REGULATION

The system operator and each onshore transmission owner are subject to regular price control reviews. This means that Ofgem approves specific revenue for each company, thereby encouraging them to improve efficiency and to keep transmission costs for electricity and gas customers low.

Ofgem has developed a new approach for setting price controls, RIIO (revenue = incentives + innovation + outputs) that will apply to the TOs from 2013 to 2021. The previous approach to regulation (RPI-X) focused on reducing costs and achieving efficiencies. The RIIO framework involves Ofgem setting a number of wider delivery outputs (with incentives/penalties attached). The RIIO approach should help ensure that energy networks are able and willing to meet the changing network challenges ahead, including playing a full role in meeting renewable energy targets to 2020 and beyond and ensuring security of supply.

NETWORK DEVELOPMENT

Transmission owners are responsible for proposing which projects should be developed. They present detailed proposals and funding requests to Ofgem, which then judges whether the proposals are in consumers' best interests, and whether the costs are efficient. Proposals also have to be approved by the appropriate Planning Authority.

Ofgem has already approved around GBP 4 billion of investment under the current extended transmission price control period which runs from 2007 to 2013. In February 2012, Ofgem published Initial Proposals to allow funding of up to GBP 7.6 billion for SPTL and SHETL in Scotland for the 2013-2021 RIIO price control period. NGET will submit its revised proposals in March 2012. NGET's original RIIO proposals to Ofgem, submitted in July 2011, contained plans for nearly GBP 17 billion of investment in new and replacement network infrastructure.

Offshore wind generation has a key part to play in meeting energy and climate change targets. Ofgem runs competitive tenders to appoint offshore transmission owners (OFTOs) to construct (where a generator chooses not to do so itself) and own and operate the offshore transmission assets (see Chapter 8 for the details). Ofgem granted four OFTO licences in 2011.

Figure 39. **Map of the electricity transmission system in Great Britain, 2010**

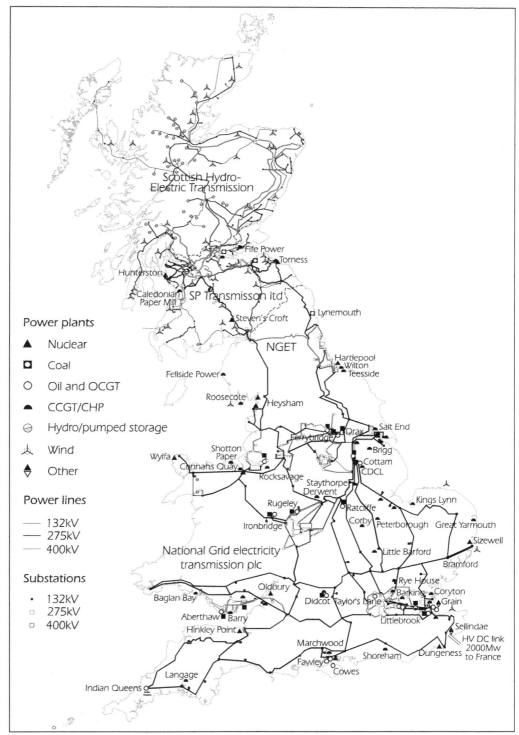

This document and any map included herein are without prejudice to the status of or sovereignty over any territory, to the delimitation of international frontiers and boundaries and to the name of any territory, city or area.

To date, the most efficient means of connecting offshore electricity generating stations has been through radial ("point-to-point") connections to shore from each electricity generating station. DECC and Ofgem recently published the findings of their joint Offshore Transmission Coordination Project[20], which sets out the case for co-ordinated offshore networks development and supports an incremental, evolutionary approach to network development rather than the building of a large-scale, meshed network from the outset. The project also identified a number of barriers to co-ordinated networks development and has put in place different measures to address these. The project findings and the measures will also help inform the potential development of any trans-national North Sea electricity grid.

The development of the offshore transmission regime in Great Britain also contributes to the North Seas Countries' Offshore Grid Initiative (NSCOGI) which aims to facilitate current and possible future grid development in the region. Offshore wind generation is expected to increase significantly in the North Sea and the Baltic Sea, from a few TWh per year today to around 125 TWh by 2020, assuming that EU member states follow their own 2010 National Renewable Energy Action Plans. In December 2010, the NSCOGI Memorandum of Understanding was signed by ten countries (Belgium, Denmark, France, Germany, Ireland, Norway, Luxembourg, the Netherlands, Sweden and the United Kingdom). Work will cover the areas of grid configuration and integration, market and regulatory issues, and planning and authorisation procedures.

INTERCONNECTIONS

The British electricity system currently has around 3.5 GW of interconnection capacity: with France (IFA), Northern Ireland (Moyle) and the Netherlands (BritNed).

The IFA (Interconnexion France-Angleterre) interconnector has a capacity of 2 GW which is allocated through long-term, day-ahead and intra-day auctions.

The Moyle interconnector has a capacity of 0.43 GW (East to West) and 0.29 GW (West to East). Capacity is allocated through long-term (1 to 3 years) and short-term (monthly) auctions. The introduction of weekly, daily and intra-day capacity products is being considered.

The BritNed interconnector has a capacity of 1 GW. Capacity is allocated with a combination of explicit and implicit auctions. The implicit auction arrangements are similar to those currently used in the Central West European market coupling (CWE) region.

Interconnection capacity is expected to increase by 0.5 GW to 4 GW in 2012 with the development of a new interconnector between Great Britain and Ireland. New interconnectors are also planned between Great Britain and France, Belgium, Norway and Ireland. Total interconnector capacity could potentially reach around 8 GW in 2020.

The launch of BritNed also saw the introduction of day-ahead market coupling with Central West Europe and is the first market coupling project in Great Britain. Market coupling through the GB-France interconnector (IFA) is planned to be commenced by the end of 2012.

---

20. http://www.decc.gov.uk/en/content/cms/meeting_energy/network/offshore_dev/offshore_dev.aspx

DISTRIBUTION

The distribution network accounts for 800 000 km of low-voltage overhead lines and underground cables (11 kV, 33 kV, 66 kV and, in England and Wales only, 132 kV). There are 14 licensed distribution network operators (DNOs), each responsible for an electricity distribution network services area. The 14 DNOs are owned by six different groups. The latest distribution price control that covers 2010-2015 has allowed about GBP 14 billion funding in the distribution network. The next distribution price control will be under the RIIO framework and run from 2015 to 2023.

PRICES

Electricity prices in Great Britain t are set by the market players either through bilateral contracts or trading in a competitive market. There are no regulated electricity prices, or price floors or ceilings for consumers or producers.

Wholesale electricity prices reflect trends in global fossil fuel prices, in particular NBP gas prices, as gas-fired plants are often the marginal generators. There have been periods of volatility in the winter of 2005 and sustained high prices throughout 2008. Since 2008 wholesale prices have been generally less volatile.

Electricity retail prices for industry fell since the introduction of competition in 1991 up to 2003. The decrease in real prices for industry was relatively smooth. Since 2003, increasing costs of wholesale electricity have pushed up industrial retail prices, peaking in 2009.

Electricity prices for households, too, fell in real terms from 1991 to 2003, but following historically low prices in 2002 and business failures, they increased to more sustainable levels. Thereafter, increasing wholesale energy costs have driven rising retail prices to their peak in 2009, before easing off in 2010. According to the UK Office for National Statistics, however, electricity prices to households rose by 14.8% from the fourth quarter of 2010 to the fourth quarter of 2011, reaching a record level. Prices to industrial customers rose on average by 6% from the third quarter of 2010 to the third quarter of 2011. Because of contract arrangements in the industry, retail prices usually follow changes in wholesale prices with a lag of at least six months.

Electricity bills consist of several components. According to Ofgem, the December 2010 bill of a typical household (with a consumption of 3 300 kWh per year) had the following breakdown: distribution and metering costs (17% of the total), transmission costs (4%), environmental costs (9%, mainly support for renewable energy and energy efficiency), and value-added tax (5%). Generation and retail costs (for example costs associated with marketing, billing and running call centres), together with the suppliers' profit margin, made up the bulk of the bill, 65%.

Figure 40. **Electricity prices in IEA member countries, 2010**

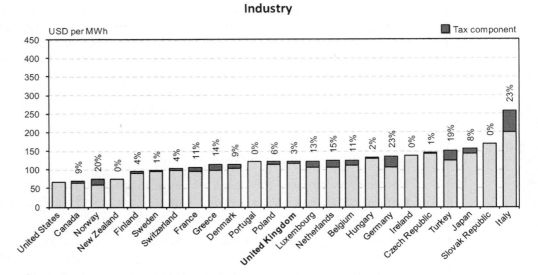

Note: Tax information is not available for the United States. Data are not available for Australia Austria, Korea and Spain.

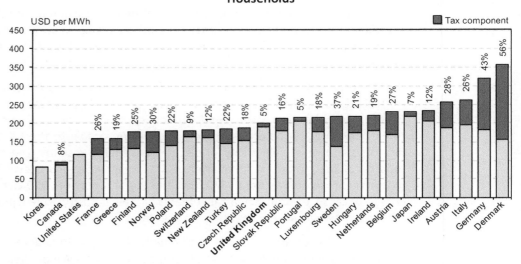

Note: Tax information is not available for Korea and the United States. Data are not available for Australia and Spain.

Source: *Energy Prices and Taxes*, IEA/OECD Paris, 2011.

By international comparison, electricity prices in the United Kingdom to industrial customers and households were at the IEA median in 2010 (see Figures 40 and 41). Taxes on electricity are relatively low. Households pay a 5% value-added tax (VAT) on electricity, while VAT is refunded to industrial customers. Since 2001, industry pays a climate change levy, currently at GBP 4.85 per MWh.

Figure 41. **Electricity prices in the United Kingdom and in selected IEA member countries, 2000 to 2010**

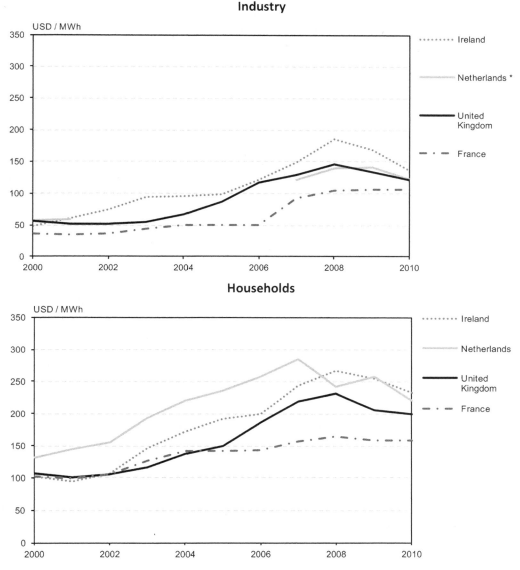

* Missing data for the Netherlands.

Source: *Energy Prices and Taxes*, IEA/OECD Paris, 2011.

CRITIQUE

The United Kingdom needs to ensure continuing reliability of its electricity systems while promoting timely decarbonisation of electricity supplies. This is the critical challenge faced by all IEA member countries. Around 19 GW of coal, oil and nuclear power capacity is scheduled to close over the next decade. Current policies are likely to deliver an outcome that would fail to meet the country's long-term climate policy targets, as new capacity is primarily gas-fired. To ensure reliability of supply and decarbonisation objectives can be met over the longer term, an efficient mix of new, cleaner generation, more efficient use of existing infrastructure and more flexible demand will be needed.

The United Kingdom will need to take effective policy action to help stimulate the needed investment in new generation and networks, improve operational performance and also encourage more efficient end-use including through more effectively harnessing demand response. The electricity market reform (EMR) is the government's main vehicle for this purpose.

ELECTRICITY MARKET REFORM

The EMR is a major change in UK energy policy. The country has been a leader in the liberalisation of energy markets. It recognised the need to identify and create structures that support the competitive development of the electricity sector, using open markets with clear price signals, high levels of liquidity and stable policy settings to attract timely and efficient investment. However, in response to ongoing delay in establishing strong market-based signals, such as the lack of a long-term carbon price under the EU-ETS, transitional interventions are needed for reaching the electricity security and decarbonisation goals in a timely manner. The EMR is discussed on a general level in the following paragraphs. Its main components are discussed in more detail in the next subsection.

The EMR proposes a transitional, targeted intervention to restructure the technology mix while simultaneously maintaining security of supply. Intervention of the kind proposed creates risk and may discourage efficient private sector responses. Hence, this should be viewed as an interim measure, with the ultimate goal of creating a more liberalised market where low-carbon generation technologies can compete to deliver innovative and least-cost outcomes. Where possible, transitional mechanisms should maintain a competitive character and be non-discriminatory between low-carbon technologies.

This intervention ultimately relies on continuing public support, and consequential multilateral political support. It is therefore essential that public discussion on the reform process is well informed. Currently, it appears that there is support for the need to diversify generation sources to provide the dual outcomes of increased energy security and reduced emissions. However, investors will ask themselves how enduring the new policies will be, if increasing resistance to rising costs is likely to emerge in the future. The government should therefore continue to communicate, in the clearest manner possible, what pathways are available to achieve energy security and decarbonisation goals, and their costs. Inclusive consultation processes are essential to encourage widest possible support and ownership of the reforms among key stakeholders and the community.

Investors need to be able to assess risk and return. Political risk for investments in long-lived power generation assets is a key consideration. It is essential that any new policy mechanisms be designed to ensure and enhance the government's standing for providing investor certainty. In particular, one should avoid the introduction of measures that are not adequately funded or supported by the Treasury, which could later require material adjustments. Given the scale of investment required to meet forecast demand growth over the long term, the rewards to the government for a reputation of delivering consistent and predictable outcomes will be substantial.

In the wider context, the outcomes of the policy initiatives proposed by the United Kingdom will be observed by both national and international stakeholders. At various times over the next decades, the proposed actions could place the United Kingdom in a position of competitive advantage or disadvantage, depending on many factors but, importantly, on the response of the European Union and other nations to climate change. The government should continue its multilateral work to develop firm and appropriately integrated international carbon pricing signals over a time-frame sufficient to adequately inform investment decisions and reduce investment risks in the electricity sector.

After addressing the need to enhance energy security, it is important that any policy mechanisms put in place to simultaneously address climate change also provide some flexibility to adapt to future unanticipated changes. Policy flexibility needs to balance the need for policy consistency to provide investor certainty, and so should only be incorporated into any policy mechanisms with great care.

NETWORK FLEXIBILITY AND INVESTMENT

With a large share of variable generation in the power plant portfolio in 2020 will come an increased need for network investment and flexibility in the balancing of supply and demand. To date, system operators and market participants have tended to use flexible conventional generation technologies for balancing purposes. However, all forms of flexibility will be needed if policy goals for electricity security and power system decarbonisation are to be simultaneously realised in a timely and least-cost manner. To this end, the United Kingdom is encouraged to consider greater and more liquid trade with adjacent markets, storage plants such as pumped hydro and especially demand-side response options.

Transmission and distribution networks and related control systems in many cases will require substantial augmentation and modernisation to support the integration of variable renewable generation in a secure and reliable manner. Concerns have been raised in several OECD countries about the slow development of the transmission systems needed to have effective access to variable renewable resources. Governments have a key role to play in helping to resolve any policy, legal or regulatory hurdles.

COMPETITION

The electricity sector in the United Kingdom has demonstrated resilience in the face of challenges such as the impacts of the financial crisis and ongoing volatility in fuel prices, delivering reliable supply at relatively competitive prices. These factors have, however, fostered the maintenance of the same industry structure that was in place at the time of the last IEA review in 2006. The market is dominated by a small number of large, vertically integrated companies that have the balance sheet, internal hedging capacity and expertise to remain robust in a volatile commercial environment.

By international comparison, liquidity in the wholesale electricity market could be higher. A higher liquidity would foster more effective risk management and price formation needed to provide a strong and credible price signal to support timely and efficient investment in power generating capacity. Such price signals would also be essential for the success of the capacity market by helping to determine a more efficient reference price for the long-term contracts proposed as part of the electricity market reform. As the government has indicated, in the absence of adequate Ofgem intervention, measures should be taken to provide stronger wholesale market liquidity, clearer pricing signals and market data, and lower barriers to entry for new entrants. The case for more targeted intervention, such as divesting, should also be considered.

To help boost competition, the government should also ensure that suppliers provide contract information to retail customers that is accurate with respect to the benefits of switching. Information transparency is a key to developing well-informed customers able to exercise choice and the emergence of retail entities that can provide the innovative products needed to help empower choice and harness demand response potential.

ELECTRICITY MARKET REFORM: KEY MECHANISMS

Turning to the EMR in more detail, integrating the four key mechanisms (discussed below) into a well-functioning market is likely to present some major issues for the United Kingdom. The IEA is impressed by the scope and the ambition of the reform and encourages the United Kingdom to accelerate early adoption of low-carbon technologies in the context of climate change and to address market imperfections. Effective implementation is likely to require the government to make difficult choices within a context of rising prices.

Carbon price floor (CPF)

The CPF is a clear and simple measure intended to correct weak market signals in a time of uncertainty about EU long-term carbon price trajectories. However, there are doubts that a major differential with EU-ETS prices can be sustained and also about government commitment to continued escalation of the price floor over the long term. Consequently, the EMR also includes contracts-for-difference feed-in tariffs to further reduce electricity price risk to investors.

As a consequence, the CPF will only affect electricity generators that are not covered by centrally allocated contracts, namely gas-fired, (non-CCS) coal-fired and existing nuclear plants. Given the differences in generating costs, the CPF can be expected to increase revenues to existing nuclear plants and to discourage the use of non-CCS coal-fired generation.

Contracts-for-difference feed-in tariffs (FiT CfDs)

The FiT CfD is intended to complement the carbon price floor. Given the need for investment in generating capacity over the next decade, it would be reasonable to develop long-term contracts to reduce exposure to wholesale market volatility and hence materially reduce investment risk for capital-intensive low-carbon technologies. To avoid any investment hiatus, the design of FiT CfDs needs to be clarified without delay.

The following points need to be considered in order to make this measure a success:

- The determination of the strike price is essential to the success of the FiT CfDs. This task is theoretically, financially and politically sensitive and needs to be handled in a competent, systematic and transparent manner, drawing on efficient, market-based price formation and price signals to the greatest extent possible.

- Introducing a fixed-price instrument into a wholesale market with free price formation will impact wholesale and retail prices and will likely increase price volatility for the part of the wholesale market that is not under the FiT CfD system.

- The impact of FiT CfDs on the wholesale market should be carefully monitored. Its impact on financial markets and its potential to help improve liquidity should be considered as part of Ofgem's work in this context.

- The July 2011 White Paper proposes technology-specific application of FiT CfDs. This may include different allocation methods (auctioning or open tariffs) and monitoring approaches. While the desire to strengthen energy security by diversifying supply is recognised, a preferred structure for the long term would be to create a level playing field to drive efficient, low-cost deployment.

- The FiT CfD mechanism is intended to last for decades and hence the term of several consecutive governments. Its effectiveness in reducing the cost of finance and encouraging the desired investment response will be determined by the extent to which it can be shielded or "ring-fenced" from political risk.

Capacity market

From an investor point of view, the proposed changes to electricity market arrangements are likely to create uncertainty and risk which may add to the cost of new investment and discourage efficiently timed and sized investment responses. Given this risk, there may be a case for some form of transitional capacity mechanism to help address any lingering concerns, especially during the implementation phase. While capacity margins are forecast to remain sufficient for the early years of this decade, the government is right to be setting out the main principles of the capacity market now, as it will likely take several years to implement the mechanism.

The implementation of the capacity market will require a clear choice from the government on the acceptable level of security of supply to minimise the risk of blackouts. It will also require robust demand and supply forecasts. Importantly, demand-side measures will be part of the capacity mechanism. The mechanism should be neutral between supply-side and demand-side solutions.

The interaction between the capacity market and the balancing mechanism, and also feed-in tariffs/renewables obligation systems will need to be clarified. Opportunities may exist for adopting a more flexible and efficient market design that combines some or all of these functions. Another important dimension is the interaction with Ofgem's proposed improvements to wholesale market liquidity. To function well, the capacity market would need a reference price for wholesale electricity to determine the payback required from generators, and this will be best determined through efficient price formation in a competitive market.

Emissions performance standard (EPS)

The EPS may not be necessary for decarbonising power generation as long as the other proposed mechanisms operate effectively. The EPS, coupled with the existing requirements that new coal-fired power stations demonstrate CCS, will improve the competitiveness of natural gas over unabated coal which is an economical way to reduce emissions in the short term.

RECOMMENDATIONS

The government of the United Kingdom should:

☐ *Continue to communicate in the clearest manner possible what pathways are available to achieve energy security and decarbonisation goals and what they cost.*

☐ *Continue to work with Ofgem to provide stronger wholesale market liquidity, clearer pricing signals and market data, and lower barriers to entry for new entrants.*

☐ *Develop interconnections with the European market to enhance security of supply and market liquidity.*

☐ *Find ways to ensure that suppliers provide contract information to retail customers that is accurate with respect to the benefits of switching.*

☐ *Continue to work in international forums to develop multilateral endorsement of firm carbon pricing signals over a time-frame sufficient to adequately inform investment decisions in the electricity sector.*

Electricity market reform

☐ *Continue to develop and implement the electricity market reform designed to accelerate the early adoption of low-carbon technologies.*

☐ *Seek to better incorporate demand-response measures into what is a mainly supply-side oriented reform.*

Contract-for-difference feed-in tariffs

☐ *Ensure that methodologies to calculate costs for FiT CfDs are robust and transparent to gain sufficient public support for the mechanism.*

☐ *Clarify how the detailed application of FiT CfDs will vary according to the group of technologies being targeted; consider ways to increase technology-neutrality over the long term to stimulate cost-effectiveness.*

☐ *Assess carefully the potential impacts of implementing FiT CfDs on CCS deployment.*

☐ *Anticipate and monitor the interaction between this mechanism, the capacity market and the wholesale market; quantify the price risk transferred to the government through this mechanism.*

☐ *Seek to inspire investor confidence by designing a strong institutional framework, providing maximum support to the system operator as the body delivering contractual terms for low-carbon generation through FiT CfDs, and ensuring decisions are transparent and technically and economically robust.*

Capacity mechanism

☐ *Seek to ensure that this mechanism provides incentives to guarantee that adequate power system operation and supply respond dynamically to increasing variability in the marketplace, including flexible generation, demand-side options, storage facilities and interconnections to adjacent markets.*

☐ *Detail the principles of the capacity market mechanism as soon as possible, given the time needed before the effects of such a reform can be obtained.*

☐ *Monitor and assess interactions with adjacent markets and develop appropriate responses to ensure compatibility with the EU internal energy market developments.*

☐ *Develop a position on reliability levels for security of supply and ensure that robust demand and supply forecasts are available to inform these decisions.*

11. ENERGY RESEARCH, DEVELOPMENT AND DEMONSTRATION

Key data (2010)

Total expenditure on energy RD&D: GBP 476 million, up 76% from 2009, with 35% allocated for renewable energy

Share in GDP: 0.32 per 1 000 units of GDP (IEA median: 0.32)

Spending per capita: USD 11.8 (IEA median: 11.0)

OVERVIEW

The United Kingdom has a greenhouse gas (GHG) emissions reduction target of 50% by 2023-2027 (the fourth carbon budget) and 80% by 2050 from 1990 levels. Low-carbon energy technologies are viewed as a critical means of realising this objective. Equally, innovation is considered an essential national competence that must be exploited to advance economic growth, competitiveness and environmental objectives. Advanced energy technology and its broad deployment are viewed as central to meet national climate change.

In order to meet national energy efficiency, renewable energy and GHG targets, the United Kingdom faces considerable pressure to broadly deploy low-carbon power and transportation technologies. The target for the share of renewable sources in gross final energy consumption in 2020 is 15%, which implies a far greater deployment of renewable energy within the power sector (see Chapter 8).

RD&D INSTITUTIONS

Many players are involved in the advanced technology and innovation agendas across the United Kingdom. Energy research, development and demonstration (RD&D) is one dimension of the innovation strategy, although it is an important element since it plays a key role in the transport, agriculture, infrastructure and rural affairs portfolios and in industrial competitiveness. Energy development, transformation and use also have significant impacts on health and the environment. The key public players and main programmes within the development and innovation cycle are depicted in Figure 42.

The **Department of Energy and Climate Change** (DECC) has a central role in the co-ordination of energy-related innovation across the government. It also operates as one of several departments with strategic interests in the overall effectiveness of the national innovation agenda. DECC also supports and demonstrates key later-stage innovative technologies relating to energy supply and efficiency. Low-carbon innovation activities also are facilitated by the **Energy Technologies Institute** and the **Carbon Trust**.

Figure 42. **Key public energy innovation programmes**

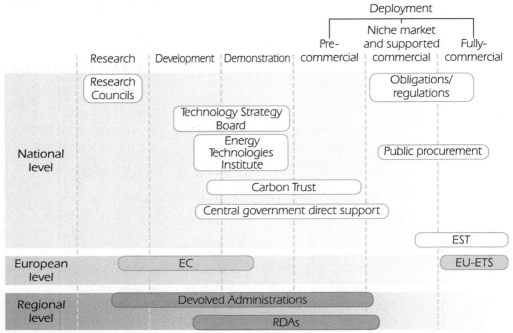

Source: Adapted from UK Environmental Transformation Fund Strategy.

Source: UK Committee on Climate Change, *Building a Low-carbon Economy – the UK's Innovation Challenge*, July 2010.

Since the 2006 IEA in-depth review, major developments within the UK innovation framework include the formation of the **Technology Strategy Board** (TSB). The TSB, which is overseen by the Department of Business, Innovation and Skills, plays a central role in the innovation strategy across the United Kingdom and financially supports medium-sized research and development (R&D) projects using technology-specific calls.

The TSB also has the task to establish and oversee a number of strategic **Technology Innovation Centres** (TICs) – to be known as Catapult Centres. These Centres are intended to create a critical mass for business and research innovation by focusing on a specific technology where there is a potentially large global market and a significant UK capability. The Centres will further bridge the gap between universities and businesses, helping to commercialise the outputs of the United Kingdom's research base. They will also allow businesses to access equipment and expertise that would otherwise be out of reach, as well as conducting their own in-house R&D.

Four Catapult Centres have been announced to date in High Value Manufacturing, Cell Therapy, Space Applications and Offshore Renewable Energy. The Offshore Renewable Energy Catapult Centre will focus on technologies applicable to offshore wind, tidal and wave power, and is anticipated to go live for business during summer 2012.

Basic research is undertaken in universities. It is co-ordinated and funded by **Research Councils UK**, which brings together the United Kingdom's seven Research Councils and has a specific Energy Programme that invests about GBP 130 million per year in multidisciplinary basic and applied research across a full spectrum of energy areas: renewables, nuclear, carbon capture and storage (CCS), low-carbon transport, as well as related social and economic policy. The design of basic science R&D funding encourages collaboration and co-ordination of research activities by academics, industry, funders and government departments.

The Research Councils UK Energy Programme aims to engage partners that can help take basic and applied research to the next stage. More than 500 public and private sector organisations are involved in energy research projects, including major energy suppliers, high-tech small and medium-sized enterprises, charities and consumer groups. The Research Councils UK's Energy Programme financially supports the **UK Energy Research Centre** (UKERC), which conducts world-class research on critical elements of sustainable future energy systems.

The **Low Carbon Innovation Coordination Group** (LCICG) brings together the key UK public sector-backed funders of low-carbon innovation. These include the Department of Energy and Climate Change, the Energy Technologies Institute, the Department of Business, Innovation and Skills, the Technology Strategy Board, Research Councils UK, the Carbon Trust, the Scottish government, Scottish Enterprise and others. The group's aim is to maximise the impact of UK public sector funding for low-carbon energy by building a shared understanding of innovation needs in the United Kingdom, by co-ordinating organisations' investment plans, by improving the communication to innovators of innovation needs and funding opportunities, and by sharing best practices and learning between organisations.

An example of the work of the group has been the development of Technology Innovation Needs Assessments (TINAs) for 10 key low-carbon technologies, such as off-shore wind, marine energy or domestic buildings energy efficiency. The TINAs aim to create a robust, shared evidence base that provides a common understanding of innovation needs in each technology sector and allows the LCICG members to assess the case for public support and to prioritise their funding decisions.

RD&D FUNDING

IEA member governments generally regard energy RD&D as an important, but future-oriented dimension of their energy policy framework. Energy RD&D covers a broad spectrum of activities, from basic research to development through technology scale-up, pilot projects, and demonstration. Publicly funded RD&D is widely recognised as a critical prerequisite for technological readiness and societal innovation within an economy. A simplified diagram of the United Kingdom's energy RD&D pathway is shown in Figure 43.

Investment in energy RD&D typically rises and falls with the perceived political importance of energy. Each IEA member country has a distinct set of energy technology priorities that largely reflect their resource base, technological competences and commercial interests. These are reflected in their energy RD&D funding allocations as illustrated in Figure 44. Over the past decade, there has been renewed interest in the energy technology field with particular emphasis on high-efficiency and low-carbon technologies reflecting growing concerns about the degree of reliance on fossil fuels and climate change.

Generally, IEA member governments have increased their energy RD&D budgets since 1997 in nominal terms. However, in real terms this spending has declined over the last 35 years. Moreover, the relative share of energy in total public RD&D has declined significantly from around 12% in 1981 to about 4% in 2008. But in the past few years some IEA member governments have clearly increased energy RD&D expenditures as shown in Figure 45.

Figure 43. **Energy RD&D pathway in the United Kingdom**

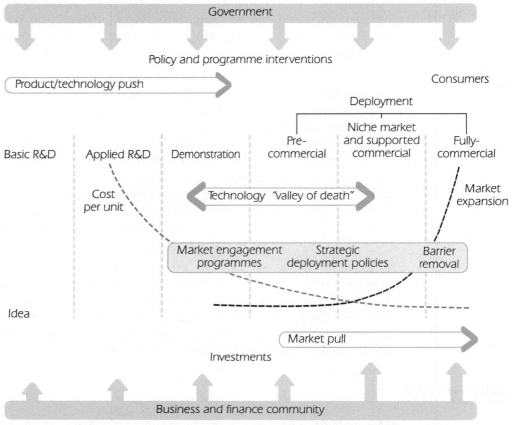

Source: Grubb M (2004), Technology Innovation and Climate Change Policy: an overview of issues and options.

Source: as quoted in *UK Committee on Climate Change, Building a Low-carbon Economy – the UK's Innovation Challenge*, July 2010.

The United Kingdom has significantly increased its commitment to energy technology advancement since 2005 and government RD&D spending is now at the IEA median on a per-GDP basis (see Figure 45). Much of this incremental funding has been directed to technology demonstration and pre-commercial deployment. It is helping to bridge the path from research to commercialisation, often called the "valley of death" in technology development and deployment. This focus reflects the political commitments taken by G8 Energy Ministers to strengthen public funding for energy efficiency and low-carbon technology development at the 2005 Gleneagles Summit, hosted by the United Kingdom, and subsequent summits.

A Spending Review undertaken in late 2010 concluded that energy RD&D continues to be a political priority. DECC has been allocated more than GBP 150 million over four years to support the development and demonstration of low-carbon energy technologies. This funding complements substantial funding allocated to energy and low-carbon RD&D through other bodies, such as the Research Councils UK and the

Technology Strategy Board. The government has also committed GBP 1 billion for early demonstration of CCS-related technologies for coal-fired power plants and potentially for gas-fired ones (see Chapter 7). DECC recognises that strategic choices are required to focus its support on those technologies where public intervention will be critical to overcome market failures and/or accelerate the realisation of the government's energy and climate change objectives.

Figure 44. **Breakdown of government spending on energy RD&D by technology area in IEA member countries, 2009**

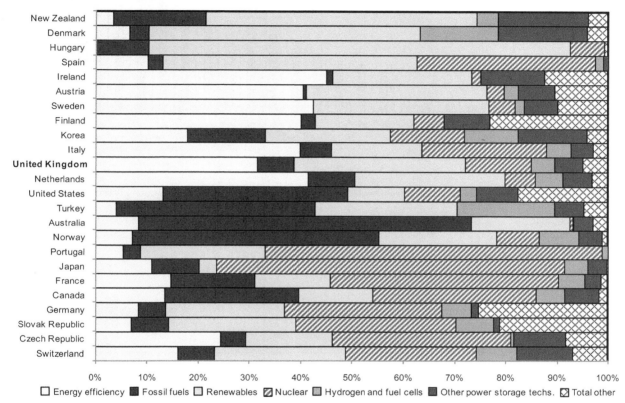

Note: Data are not available for Belgium, Greece, Luxembourg and Poland. Countries are grouped according to similarity in relative spending per technology area.

Source: *OECD Economic Outlook*, OECD Paris, 2011.

Figure 45. **Government spending on energy RD&D per GDP in IEA member countries, 2005 to 2007 and 2010**

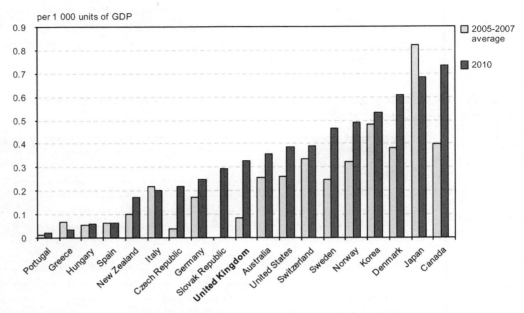

Note: Data for 2005-2007 are not available for the Slovak Republic. Data for 2010 are not available for Austria, Belgium, Finland, France, Ireland, Luxembourg, Netherlands, Poland and Turkey.

Source: IEA statistics.

Figure 46. **Government energy RD&D expenditures, 1990 to 2010**

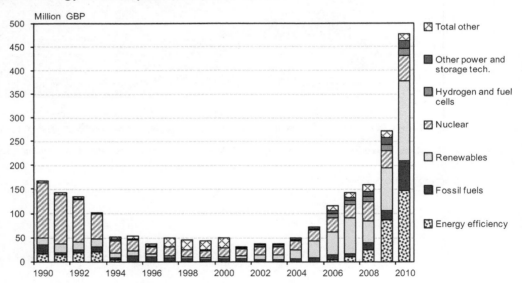

Sources: *OECD Economic Outlook*, OECD Paris, 2011 and country submission.

INTERNATIONAL COLLABORATION

The United Kingdom is an active participant within the European Union and continues to support technology advancement efforts across Europe (Box 5) and more broadly through multilateral collaboration, including participation in many IEA implementing agreements. A number of other initiatives include UK involvement such as the International Renewable Energy Agency, the International Partnership for Energy Efficiency Co-operation, the Carbon Sequestration Leadership Forum, the Renewable Energy and Energy Efficiency Partnership (REEEP), the Clean Energy Ministerial, the Global Methane Initiative and the Global Bio-energy Partnership. It also participates in many bilateral initiatives, including active partnerships with developing economies to foster their modernisation and low-carbon development plans.

The United Kingdom also continues to contribute to the Climate Investment Funds administered by the World Bank. In 2010/11, the United Kingdom contributed GBP 155 million to the Clean Technology Fund and GBP 35 million to the Scaling Up Renewable Energy Programme.

Box 5. **EU Framework Programme and the SET Plan**

The United Kingdom's energy RD&D investments both support and are influenced by the EU 7th Framework Programme for R&D (2007 to 2013) and the EU Strategic Energy Technology (SET) Plan. Specific technology priorities under the SET Plan do not differ substantially from those of the United Kingdom.

As noted in the European Commission's 2009 communication regarding the SET Plan:

"One of the EU's key ambitions is to develop a low-carbon economy. The EU has put in place a comprehensive policy framework, including climate and energy targets for 2020, a carbon price, among others, and a programme to accelerate development of those technologies with the greatest potential, as energy markets on their own will not deliver decarbonisation in the time-frames necessary.... What is also clear is that technology and the efficient use of resources lie at the heart of the challenge.... We need to stimulate our best brains to find new and better ways of producing and consuming energy."

As part of the SET Plan, the EU has established a series of European Industrial Initiatives (EIIs) as well as a European Energy Research Alliance to help accelerate the development of these technologies. EIIs have been established for wind, solar, electricity grids and CCS as well as smart cities (energy efficiency), nuclear fission and bioenergy. The United Kingdom both actively participates in and receives funding through these initiatives. The United Kingdom also actively encourages deeper co-operation between EU energy technology development initiatives and those of the IEA and other international organisations.

CRITIQUE

The government's recent increase in investment in energy RD&D, relative to investment levels over the past 20 years, is encouraging. All of the elements of a solid energy RD&D strategy for the United Kingdom have recently been discussed in various forums. These include studies and reports of the Committee on Climate Change; DECC reviews and strategies; the LCICG's Technology Innovation Needs Assessments; reviews undertaken by the National Audit Office; the work programme and annual report of the UKERC; and the strategies and business plans of the Energy Technologies Institute, the Technology Strategy Board and its Catapult Centres.

It would be helpful to distil these ideas and initiatives into a comprehensive energy RD&D strategy that is used to both leverage available funding and enhance coherence to the multitude of related activities under way domestically and internationally. It likely will be a considerable challenge to pull these many pieces together where government mandates and engagement span multiple departments. In coalescing this strategy, DECC should clearly articulate both short- and long-term technology development objectives, set milestones with some degree of specificity to help align activities and planned spending. This observation was fairly central to the Committee on Climate Change's 2010 report *Building a Low-carbon Economy*, which noted the need for a long-term strategy that looks to advance specific energy technologies to 2050 and beyond. The report also called for greater clarity on both the objectives for the delivering agents within the RD&D system and the desired outcomes that can be effectively monitored and evaluated to ensure public value for money.

That report also presented sound analysis of the United Kingdom's strengths and weaknesses in specific technology domains. It categorised various technology areas as being appropriate to undertake strategies related to R&D, development and deployment, or solely deployment. The report clearly concludes that the United Kingdom is well positioned to lead in selected technology development as well as in RD&D.

Energy RD&D holds considerable long-term potential as a catalyst for new technologies that are both clean and low-carbon. While the promise is significant, technology development and advancement requires substantial investments of both human and financial resources and generally long lead times. Success requires long-term strategic focus, patient but demanding capital, and effective use of human resources in seeking and leveraging competitive advantages that reflect national circumstances. The most successful countries in technological innovation have effective approaches that align incentives and efforts across the innovation chain. Recent commitments by the leading technology development players, including the United States, China, Germany and Japan indicate that the investment levels are accelerating, as are the stakes in moving towards low-carbon development. Since its market liberalisation in the early 1990s, the United Kingdom government has been a modest investor in energy RD&D and has largely divested its interest in publicly funded energy labs. However, today among the IEA countries, the United Kingdom ranks close to the median both in terms of absolute and per-capita spending on energy RD&D.

The levels of spending do not seem to match the United Kingdom's ambitious climate policy objectives and its world-renowned academic institutions and capability. The United Kingdom has leading-edge capability in offshore wind, tidal, wave, CCS, electric vehicles and the nuclear supply chain. While funding in these areas continues, including the billion-pound commitment to demonstrate CCS technology deployment within the power sector, it is not always clear what specific objectives are being pursued through energy R&D or how effectively the public monies are spent.

Since the 2006 in-depth review, the United Kingdom has made progress in responding to IEA recommendations and has clarified the roles and responsibilities of relevant stakeholders within the energy innovation chain. The need to innovate and to accelerate the deployment of advanced low-carbon technologies is well recognised. Further steps do need to be taken across the innovation system to strengthen the delivery of direct public support for low-carbon technology development, adaptation, demonstration and deployment. DECC recognises the need to strengthen the strategic focus and improve co-ordination among the relevant innovation and RD&D landscapes, as well as to pursue best practices. These are in keeping with the findings and recommendations of the recent National Audit Office review of renewables RD&D activities. The DECC-led cross-departmental Review of Low Carbon Innovation Delivery took on board those findings and developed a plan of work that will be delivered by the Low Carbon Innovation Coordination Group in 2012.

In working towards a more strategic and focused approach, the relevant players are developing an evidence base to better understand the inherent capabilities and effectiveness of current efforts. In partnership with the Low Carbon Innovation Coordination Group, efforts are being directed at developing a number of technology innovation needs assessments to clarify and prioritise next steps. These efforts are commendable and should help DECC and others across the UK innovation system to develop and execute a coherent strategy that will make effective use of both human and fiscal resources in advancing promising technologies and the UK industrial capability in the transition to a low-carbon economy.

Given the distribution of required expertise across the globe, international collaboration can help and may be essential to accelerate technology development by leveraging available intellectual capital, sharing commercial risk, lowering costs and shortening development cycle times to develop advanced energy technologies.

RECOMMENDATIONS

The government of the United Kingdom should:

☐ *Consider developing an ambitious technology innovation strategy which leverages the country's academic and institutional capabilities to develop selected low-carbon technologies.*

☐ *As part of this strategy, acknowledge and publicly fund at world-class levels a focused energy RD&D programme to catalyse a broader United Kingdom innovation agenda that reflects the country's industrial and intellectual comparative advantage.*

☐ *Continue to participate actively in international RD&D collaboration to share both costs and risks, accelerate technology development and diffusion, and help communicate broadly the lessons learned across this network.*

**PART IV
ANNEXES**

ANNEX A: ORGANISATION OF THE REVIEW

REVIEW CRITERIA

The Shared Goals, which were adopted by the IEA Ministers at their 4 June 1993 meeting in Paris, provide the evaluation criteria for the in-depth reviews conducted by the IEA. The Shared Goals are presented in Annex C.

REVIEW TEAM AND PREPARATION OF THE REPORT

The in-depth review team visited the United Kingdom from 6 to 10 June 2011. The team met with government officials, energy suppliers, interest groups and various other organisations. This report was drafted on the basis of these meetings, the team's preliminary assessment of the UK energy policy, the government response to the IEA energy policy questionnaire and other information.

The members of the team were:

IEA member countries

Mr. Pierre-Marie ABADIE, France (team leader)

Dr. Charlotte BILLGREN, Sweden

Mr. Espen HAUGE, Norway

Mr. Aurél KENESSEY, the Netherlands

Ms. Phyllis ODENBACH SUTTON, Canada

Mr. Peter WILSON, Australia

European Commission

Mr. Marcus LIPPOLD

OECD Nuclear Energy Agency

Dr. Jan Horst KEPPLER

International Energy Agency

Mr. Robert ARNOT

Mr. Hugo CHANDLER

Mr. Shinji FUJINO

Mr. Dennis VOLK

Mr. Miika TOMMILA (desk officer)

The team is grateful for the co-operation and assistance of the many people it met during the visit, the kind hospitality and the willingness to discuss the challenges and opportunities that the United Kingdom is currently facing. The team wishes to express its sincere appreciation to Mr. Simon Virley, Director General, and his staff at the Department of Energy and Climate Change for their hospitality and personal engagement in briefing the team on energy policy issues. In particular, the team wishes to thank Ms. Claire Ball and Dr. Matthew Clarke for their unfailing helpfulness in preparing for and guiding the visit, and Dr. Chris Snary for his dedication displayed as the contact person for finalising the review process.

Miika Tommila managed the review and drafted Chapters 1 to 5 and Chapter 10 of the report. Other chapters were drafted by Anne-Sophie Corbeau (natural gas section in Chapter 5), Dennis Volk (Chapter 6), Matthias Finkenrath (Chapter 7), Hugo Chandler (Chapter 8), Jan Horst Keppler (Chapter 9) and Robert Arnot (Chapter 11). Georg Bussmann drafted statistics-related sections for most chapters. Helpful comments were provided by the review team members and many IEA colleagues, including André Aasrud, Manuel Baritaud, Richard Baron, Ulrich Benterbusch, Sara Bryan Pasquier, Doug Cooke, Carlos Fernandez Alvarez, Shinji Fujino, Rebecca Gaghen, Christina Hood, Juho Lipponen, Kieran McNamara, Carrie Pottinger, Andrew Robertson and Laszlo Varro.

Georg Bussmann and Bertrand Sadin prepared the figures. Karen Treanton, Davide D'Ambrosio and Raphael Vial provided support on statistics. Muriel Custodio, Jane Barbière and Astrid Dumond managed the production process. Debra Justus and Viviane Consoli provided editorial assistance. Marilyn Ferris helped in the final stages of preparation.

ORGANISATIONS VISITED

During its visit to the United Kingdom, the review team met with the following organisations:

Association of Electricity Producers

BP

Carbon Trust

Centrica

CoalPro

Consumer Focus

Department of Energy and Climate Change

Department of Transport

EDF

Energy Saving Trust

E3G

Green Alliance

National Grid

Nuclear Industry Association

Ofgem

Oil & Gas UK

Renewable Energy Association

RenewableUK

Shell

UK Business Council for Sustainable Energy

UK Energy Research Council

ANNEX B:
ENERGY BALANCES
AND KEY STATISTICAL DATA

Unit: Mtoe

SUPPLY		1973	1990	2000	2009	2010	2020	2030
TOTAL PRODUCTION		**108.5**	**208.0**	**272.5**	**158.9**	**148.8**	**122.0**	..
Coal		75.9	53.6	18.7	10.7	11.0	10.5	..
Peat		-	-	-	-	-	-	-
Oil		0.6	95.2	131.7	70.9	64.4	41.1	24.6
Natural Gas		24.4	40.9	97.5	53.7	51.5	34.4	21.9
Biofuels & Waste[1]		-	0.6	1.9	4.3	4.4	22.4	22.4
Nuclear		7.3	17.1	22.2	18.0	16.2	6.8	25.5
Hydro		0.3	0.4	0.4	0.5	0.3	0.4	0.4
Wind		-	0.0	0.1	0.8	0.9	6.5	8.2
Geothermal		-	0.0	0.0	0.0	0.0	-	-
Solar		-	0.0	0.0	0.1	0.1	0.0	0.0
TOTAL NET IMPORTS[2]		**107.7**	**-4.1**	**-52.9**	**41.5**	**47.8**	**54.7**	**-20.9**
Coal	Exports	2.0	1.8	0.8	0.6	0.9	-	-
	Imports	1.1	10.3	15.2	23.6	16.6	10.9	..
	Net Imports	-0.9	8.5	14.5	23.0	15.7	10.9	..
Oil	Exports	20.7	76.2	117.4	72.9	69.6	-	-
	Imports	136.7	65.2	70.6	79.0	80.9	29.8	51.7
	Int'l Marine and Aviation Bunkers	-8.0	-8.9	-12.5	-13.6	-12.8	-16.4	-20.3
	Net Imports	107.9	-19.9	-59.2	-7.5	-1.6	13.4	31.4
Natural Gas	Exports	-	-	11.3	10.6	13.6	-	-
	Imports	0.7	6.2	2.0	35.3	45.6	29.9	43.6
	Net Imports	0.7	6.2	-9.3	24.7	32.0	29.9	43.6
Electricity	Exports	0.0	0.0	0.0	0.3	0.4	0.6	0.6
	Imports	0.0	1.0	1.2	0.6	0.6	1.1	1.1
	Net Imports	0.0	1.0	1.2	0.2	0.2	0.5	0.5
TOTAL STOCK CHANGES		**1.8**	**2.0**	**3.3**	**-3.4**	**5.9**	**-**	**-**
TOTAL SUPPLY (TPES)[3]		**218.1**	**205.9**	**222.9**	**197.1**	**202.5**	**176.7**	**188.9**
Coal		76.4	63.1	36.5	29.8	30.7	21.3	10.5
Peat		-	-	-	-	-	-	-
Oil		108.9	76.4	73.2	64.2	63.4	54.5	55.9
Natural Gas		25.1	47.2	87.4	78.1	84.8	64.3	65.5
Biofuels & Waste[1]		-	0.6	1.9	5.4	5.9	22.4	22.4
Nuclear		7.3	17.1	22.2	18.0	16.2	6.8	25.5
Hydro		0.3	0.4	0.4	0.5	0.3	0.4	0.4
Wind		-	0.0	0.1	0.8	0.9	6.5	8.2
Geothermal		-	0.0	0.0	0.0	0.0	-	-
Solar		-	0.0	0.0	0.1	0.1	0.0	0.0
Electricity Trade[4]		0.0	1.0	1.2	0.2	0.2	0.5	0.5
Shares (%)								
Coal		*35.0*	*30.6*	*16.4*	*15.1*	*15.2*	*12.1*	*5.5*
Peat		*-*	*-*	*-*	*-*	*-*	*-*	*-*
Oil		*49.9*	*37.1*	*32.8*	*32.6*	*31.3*	*30.8*	*29.6*
Natural Gas		*11.5*	*22.9*	*39.2*	*39.6*	*41.9*	*36.4*	*34.7*
Biofuels & Waste		*-*	*0.3*	*0.9*	*2.7*	*2.9*	*12.6*	*11.9*
Nuclear		*3.3*	*8.3*	*9.9*	*9.1*	*8.0*	*3.8*	*13.5*
Hydro		*0.2*	*0.2*	*0.2*	*0.2*	*0.2*	*0.2*	*0.2*
Wind		*-*	*-*	*-*	*0.4*	*0.4*	*3.7*	*4.3*
Geothermal		*-*	*-*	*-*	*-*	*-*	*-*	*-*
Solar		*-*	*-*	*-*	*-*	*-*	*-*	*-*
Electricity Trade		*-*	*0.5*	*0.5*	*0.1*	*0.1*	*0.3*	*0.3*

0 is negligible, - is nil, .. is not available

Forecast data for heat are not available. Forecast imports for oil and natural gas are actually net imports.
Forecasts for production and trade of coal are not available.

Unit: Mtoe

DEMAND							
FINAL CONSUMPTION	1973	1990	2000	2009	2010	2020	2030
TFC	**143.2**	**137.8**	**150.5**	**131.5**	**137.9**	**126.0**	**130.7**
Coal	31.7	10.8	4.1	2.8	2.8	2.0	2.0
Peat	-	-	-	-	-	-	-
Oil	73.1	61.2	62.6	55.9	56.3	48.5	49.2
Natural Gas	18.4	41.8	52.4	41.8	47.1	38.1	40.4
Biofuels & Waste[1]	-	0.4	0.6	1.9	2.1	10.0	8.5
Geothermal	-	0.0	0.0	0.0	0.0	-	-
Solar	-	0.0	0.0	0.1	0.1	-	-
Electricity	20.0	23.6	28.3	27.8	28.2	27.3	30.7
Heat	-	-	2.4	1.2	1.3	..	..
Shares (%)							
Coal	*22.1*	*7.8*	*2.7*	*2.2*	*2.0*	*1.6*	*1.5*
Peat	*-*	*-*	*-*	*-*	*-*	*-*	*-*
Oil	*51.0*	*44.4*	*41.6*	*42.5*	*40.8*	*38.5*	*37.6*
Natural Gas	*12.8*	*30.3*	*34.8*	*31.8*	*34.1*	*30.2*	*30.9*
Biofuels & Waste	*-*	*0.3*	*0.4*	*1.4*	*1.6*	*8.0*	*6.5*
Geothermal	*-*	*-*	*-*	*-*	*-*	*-*	*-*
Solar	*-*	*-*	*-*	*0.1*	*0.1*	*-*	*-*
Electricity	*14.0*	*17.1*	*18.8*	*21.1*	*20.5*	*21.7*	*23.5*
Heat	*-*	*-*	*1.6*	*0.9*	*0.9*	*..*	*..*
TOTAL INDUSTRY[5]	**64.6**	**42.7**	**45.2**	**33.6**	**34.5**	**38.5**	**37.8**
Coal	14.0	6.4	2.5	2.2	2.1	1.3	1.0
Peat	-	-	-	-	-	-	-
Oil	33.3	15.6	16.3	12.0	12.1	13.2	12.9
Natural Gas	9.4	12.0	15.3	9.6	10.1	9.9	9.4
Biofuels & Waste[1]	-	0.1	0.3	0.4	0.4	3.8	3.8
Geothermal	-	-	-	-	. -	-	-
Solar	-	-	-	-	-	-	-
Electricity	7.8	8.7	9.8	8.7	9.0	10.3	10.8
Heat	-	-	1.1	0.8	0.8	..	..
Shares (%)							
Coal	*21.7*	*15.0*	*5.5*	*6.5*	*6.1*	*3.3*	*2.7*
Peat	*-*	*-*	*-*	*-*	*-*	*-*	*-*
Oil	*51.5*	*36.5*	*36.0*	*35.7*	*35.0*	*34.3*	*34.0*
Natural Gas	*14.6*	*28.0*	*33.7*	*28.6*	*29.2*	*25.7*	*24.9*
Biofuels & Waste	*-*	*0.2*	*0.6*	*1.1*	*1.2*	*9.8*	*9.9*
Geothermal	*-*	*-*	*-*	*-*	*-*	*-*	*-*
Solar	*-*	*-*	*-*	*-*	*-*	*-*	*-*
Electricity	*12.2*	*20.3*	*21.7*	*25.8*	*26.0*	*26.9*	*28.5*
Heat	*-*	*-*	*2.4*	*2.3*	*2.4*	*..*	*..*
TRANSPORT[3]	**27.6**	**39.2**	**41.9**	**41.2**	**41.3**	**37.2**	**36.9**
OTHER[6]	**51.0**	**56.0**	**63.4**	**56.6**	**62.1**	**50.3**	**56.0**
Coal	17.6	4.4	1.6	0.7	0.7	0.8	1.0
Peat	-	-	-	-	-	-	-
Oil	12.4	6.9	5.2	4.0	4.4	1.5	1.3
Natural Gas	9.0	29.8	37.2	32.2	37.0	28.2	31.0
Biofuels & Waste[1]	-	0.3	0.3	0.5	0.6	3.3	3.2
Geothermal	-	0.0	0.0	0.0	0.0	-	-
Solar	-	0.0	0.0	0.1	0.1	-	-
Electricity	12.0	14.5	17.8	18.7	18.9	16.6	19.6
Heat	-	-	1.3	0.4	0.4	..	..
Shares (%)							
Coal	*34.6*	*7.9*	*2.5*	*1.2*	*1.1*	*1.5*	*1.7*
Peat	*-*	*-*	*-*	*-*	*-*	*-*	*-*
Oil	*24.4*	*12.4*	*8.1*	*7.0*	*7.0*	*2.9*	*2.3*
Natural Gas	*17.6*	*53.3*	*58.6*	*56.9*	*59.6*	*56.0*	*55.2*
Biofuels & Waste	*-*	*0.6*	*0.5*	*0.9*	*1.0*	*6.5*	*5.7*
Geothermal	*-*	*-*	*-*	*-*	*-*	*-*	*-*
Solar	*-*	*-*	*-*	*0.1*	*0.1*	*-*	*-*
Electricity	*23.5*	*25.9*	*28.0*	*33.1*	*30.5*	*33.0*	*35.0*
Heat	*-*	*-*	*2.1*	*0.8*	*0.7*	*..*	*..*

Unit: Mtoe

DEMAND							
ENERGY TRANSFORMATION AND LOSSES	1973	1990	2000	2009	2010	2020	2030
ELECTRICITY GENERATION[7]							
INPUT (Mtoe)	72.4	73.8	81.7	78.5	78.6	64.8	75.5
OUTPUT (Mtoe)	24.2	27.3	32.2	32.1	32.5	30.4	34.1
(TWh gross)	281.4	317.8	374.4	373.1	378.0	353.0	396.9
Output Shares (%)							
Coal	*62.1*	*65.0*	*32.7*	*28.0*	*28.8*	*20.6*	*6.0*
Peat	*-*	*-*	*-*	*-*	*-*	*-*	*-*
Oil	*25.6*	*10.9*	*2.3*	*1.6*	*1.3*	*0.8*	*0.6*
Natural Gas	*1.0*	*1.6*	*39.6*	*44.6*	*46.3*	*38.1*	*33.3*
Biofuels & Waste	*-*	*0.2*	*1.2*	*3.3*	*3.5*	*10.1*	*10.3*
Nuclear	*10.0*	*20.7*	*22.7*	*18.5*	*16.4*	*7.4*	*24.6*
Hydro	*1.4*	*1.6*	*1.4*	*1.4*	*1.0*	*1.3*	*1.2*
Wind	*-*	*-*	*0.3*	*2.5*	*2.7*	*21.6*	*23.9*
Geothermal	*-*	*-*	*-*	*-*	*-*	*-*	*-*
Solar	*-*	*-*	*-*	*-*	*-*	*-*	*-*
TOTAL LOSSES	76.5	68.4	72.4	65.3	64.6	50.8	58.2
of which:							
Electricity and Heat Generation[8]	48.2	46.5	47.1	45.1	44.7	34.4	41.3
Other Transformation	11.0	5.4	5.8	3.2	2.7	1.7	1.7
Own Use and Losses[9]	17.3	16.4	19.5	16.9	17.3	14.6	15.2
Statistical Differences	-1.7	-0.2	0.1	0.3	-0.0	-	-
INDICATORS	1973	1990	2000	2009	2010	2020	2030
GDP (billion 2005 USD)	1118.60	1569.13	2015.53	2287.80	2318.77	2810.22	3392.21
Population (millions)	56.22	57.24	58.89	61.79	62.26	64.45	66.83
TPES/GDP[10]	0.20	0.13	0.11	0.09	0.09	0.06	0.06
Energy Production/TPES	0.50	1.01	1.22	0.81	0.74	0.69	..
Per Capita TPES[11]	3.88	3.60	3.79	3.19	3.25	2.74	2.83
Oil Supply/GDP[10]	0.10	0.05	0.04	0.03	0.03	0.02	0.02
TFC/GDP[10]	0.13	0.09	0.08	0.06	0.06	0.05	0.04
Per Capita TFC[11]	2.55	2.41	2.56	2.13	2.22	1.95	1.96
Energy-related CO_2 Emissions (Mt CO_2)[12]	636.7	549.3	524.3	465.5	483.5	377.8	343.0
CO_2 Emissions from Bunkers (Mt CO_2)	25.0	26.7	37.4	40.7	38.4	49.0	60.6
GROWTH RATES (% per year)	73-79	79-90	90-00	00-09	09-10	10-20	20-30
TPES	-0.1	-0.5	0.8	-1.4	2.8	-1.4	0.7
Coal	-0.5	-1.5	-5.3	-2.2	3.1	-3.6	-6.9
Peat	-	-	-	-	-	-	-
Oil	-2.8	-1.7	-0.4	-1.5	-1.3	-1.5	0.3
Natural Gas	8.3	1.4	6.4	-1.2	8.6	-2.7	0.2
Biofuels & Waste	-	-	11.9	12.1	9.7	14.2	0.0
Nuclear	5.4	5.0	2.6	-2.3	-10.1	-8.3	14.2
Hydro	1.6	1.9	-0.2	0.4	-31.6	2.8	-0.0
Wind	-	-	55.2	29.0	9.5	22.3	2.2
Geothermal	-	-	-	-	-	-100.0	-
Solar	-	-	1.0	23.0	26.8	-31.7	-
TFC	0.1	-0.4	0.9	-1.5	4.9	-0.9	0.4
Electricity Consumption	0.9	1.0	1.8	-0.2	1.7	-0.3	1.2
Energy Production	10.1	0.7	2.7	-5.8	-6.4	-2.0	..
Net Oil Imports	-29.1	..	..	..	..	..	8.8
GDP	1.5	2.3	2.5	1.4	1.4	1.9	1.9
Growth in the TPES/GDP Ratio	-1.5	-2.7	-1.6	-2.8	1.2	-3.2	-1.2
Growth in the TFC/GDP Ratio	-1.3	-2.6	-1.6	-3.0	3.5	-2.7	-1.4

Please note: Rounding may cause totals to differ from the sum of the elements.

Footnotes to energy balances and key statistical data

1. Biofuels and waste comprises solid biofuels, liquid biofuels, biogases, industrial waste and municipal waste. Data are often based on partial surveys and may not be comparable between countries.

2. In addition to coal, oil, natural gas and electricity, total net imports also include biofuels.

3. Excludes international marine bunkers and international aviation bunkers.

4. Total supply of electricity represents net trade. A negative number in the share of TPES indicates that exports are greater than imports.

5. Industry includes non-energy use.

6. Other includes residential, commercial, public services, agriculture, forestry, fishing and other non-specified.

7. Inputs to electricity generation include inputs to electricity, CHP and heat plants. Output refers only to electricity generation.

8. Losses arising in the production of electricity and heat at main activity producer utilities and autoproducers. For non-fossil-fuel electricity generation, theoretical losses are shown based on plant efficiencies of approximately 33% for nuclear and 100% for hydro, wind and photovoltaic.

9. Data on "losses" for forecast years often include large statistical differences covering differences between expected supply and demand and mostly do not reflect real expectations on transformation gains and losses.

10. Toe per thousand US dollars at 2005 prices and exchange rates.

11. Toe per person.

12. "Energy-related CO_2 emissions" have been estimated using the IPCC Tier I Sectoral Approach from the *Revised 1996 IPCC Guidelines*. In accordance with the IPCC methodology, emissions from international marine and aviation bunkers are not included in national totals. Projected emissions for oil and gas are derived by calculating the ratio of emissions to energy use for 2009 and applying this factor to forecast energy supply. Future coal emissions are based on product-specific supply projections and are calculated using the IPCC/OECD emission factors and methodology.

ANNEX C: INTERNATIONAL ENERGY AGENCY "SHARED GOALS"

The member countries* of the International Energy Agency (IEA) seek to create conditions in which the energy sectors of their economies can make the fullest possible contribution to sustainable economic development and to the well-being of their people and of the environment. In formulating energy policies, the establishment of free and open markets is a fundamental point of departure, though energy security and environmental protection need to be given particular emphasis by governments. IEA countries recognise the significance of increasing global interdependence in energy. They therefore seek to promote the effective operation of international energy markets and encourage dialogue with all participants. In order to secure their objectives, member countries therefore aim to create a policy framework consistent with the following goals:

1. Diversity, efficiency and flexibility within the energy sector are basic conditions for longer-term energy security: the fuels used within and across sectors and the sources of those fuels should be as diverse as practicable. Non-fossil fuels, particularly nuclear and hydro power, make a substantial contribution to the energy supply diversity of IEA countries as a group.

2. Energy systems should have **the ability to respond promptly and flexibly to energy emergencies.** In some cases this requires collective mechanisms and action: IEA countries co-operate through the Agency in responding jointly to oil supply emergencies.

3. The environmentally sustainable provision and use of energy are central to the achievement of these shared goals. Decision-makers should seek to minimise the adverse environmental impacts of energy activities, just as environmental decisions should take account of the energy consequences. Government interventions should respect the Polluter Pays Principle where practicable.

4. More environmentally acceptable energy sources need to be encouraged and developed. Clean and efficient use of fossil fuels is essential. The development of economic non-fossil sources is also a priority. A number of IEA member countries wish to retain and improve the nuclear option for the future, at the highest available safety standards, because nuclear energy does not emit carbon dioxide. Renewable sources will also have an increasingly important contribution to make.

5. Improved energy efficiency can promote both environmental protection and energy security in a cost-effective manner. There are significant opportunities for greater energy efficiency at all stages of the energy cycle from production to consumption. Strong efforts by governments and all energy users are needed to realise these opportunities.

6. Continued **research, development and market deployment of new and improved energy technologies** make a critical contribution to achieving the objectives outlined above. Energy technology policies should complement broader energy policies. International co-operation in the development and dissemination of energy technologies, including industry participation and co-operation with non-member countries, should be encouraged.

7. Undistorted energy prices enable markets to work efficiently. Energy prices should not be held artificially below the costs of supply to promote social or industrial goals. To the extent necessary and practicable, the environmental costs of energy production and use should be reflected in prices.

8. Free and open trade and a secure framework for investment contribute to efficient energy markets and energy security. Distortions to energy trade and investment should be avoided.

9. Co-operation among all energy market participants helps to improve information and understanding, and encourages the development of efficient, environmentally acceptable and flexible energy systems and markets worldwide. These are needed to help promote the investment, trade and confidence necessary to achieve global energy security and environmental objectives.

(The "Shared Goals" were adopted by IEA Ministers at the meeting of 4 June 1993 Paris, France.)

*Australia, Austria, Belgium, Canada, the Czech Republic, Denmark, Finland, France, Germany, Greece, Hungary, Ireland, Italy, Japan, Korea, Luxembourg, the Netherlands, New Zealand, Norway, Poland, Portugal, the Slovak Republic, Spain, Sweden, Switzerland, Turkey, the United Kingdom, the United States.

ANNEX D: GLOSSARY AND LIST OF ABBREVIATIONS

In this report, abbreviations and acronyms are substituted for a number of terms used within the International Energy Agency. While these terms generally have been written out on first mention, this glossary provides a quick and central reference for many of the abbreviations used.

b/d	barrels per day
bcm	billion cubic metres
CCGT	combined-cycle gas turbine
CCS	carbon capture and storage
CHP	combined production of heat and power
DECC	Department of Energy and Climate Change
DSO	distribution system operator
EIA	environmental impact assessment
EMR	electricity market reform
EPS	emissions performance standard
EU	European Union
GDP	gross domestic product
GHG	greenhouse gas
GW	gigawatt, or 1 watt x 10^9
GWh	gigawatt-hour, or 1 gigawatt x 1 hour
IEA	International Energy Agency
IGCC	integrated gas combined cycle
IPCC	Intergovernmental Panel on Climate Change
kb	thousand barrels
kt	kilotonne
ktoe	thousand tonnes of oil equivalent; see toe
kW	kilowatt, or 1 watt x 10^3
kWh	kilowatt-hour, or 1 kilowatt x 1 hour
kV	kilovolt, or 1 volt x 10^3

LNG liquefied natural gas

m metre
m^2 square metre
MBtu million British thermal units
mcm million cubic metres
MEP minimum energy performance
Mt million tonnes
Mtoe million tonnes of oil equivalent; see toe
MW megawatt, or 1 watt x 10^6
MWh megawatt-hour, or 1 megawatt x 1 hour

NBP National Balancing Point
NEEAP National Energy Efficiency Action Plan

Ofgem Office of Gas and Electricity Markets (the regulator)

PPP purchasing power parity: the rate of currency conversion that equalises the purchasing power of different currencies, *i.e.* estimates the differences in price levels between different countries
PV photovoltaic

RD&D research, development and demonstration

TFC total final consumption of energy
toe tonne of oil equivalent, defined as 10^7 kcal
TPA third-party access
TPES total primary energy supply
TSO transmission system operator
TW terawatt, or 1 watt x 10^{12}
TWh terawatt-hour, or 1 terawatt x 1 hour

UNFCCC United Nations Framework Convention on Climate Change

VAT value-added tax

International Energy Agency

Online bookshop

IEA PUBLICATIONS, 9, RUE DE LA FÉDÉRATION, 75739 PARIS CEDEX 15
PRINTED IN FRANCE BY SOREGRAPH, APRIL 2012
(61 2012 02 1P1) ISBN: 9789264170865